HRH The Duchess of Kent, Controller Commandant from 1967

The Women's Royal Army Corps

The Women's Royal Army Corps

by Shelford Bidwell

Leo Cooper Ltd, London

First published in Great Britain 1977 by
LEO COOPER LTD.
196 Shaftesbury Avenue
London WC2H 8JL

Copyright © 1977 by Shelford Bidwell

ISBN 0 85052 099 1

Printed in Great Britain by
Ebenezer Baylis & Son Ltd
The Trinity Press, Worcester, and London

For P.J.L.

Contents

Illustrations

Acknowledgments

I must first record my indebtedness to Colonel J. M. Cowper TD, late WRAC, who wrote the book on Queen Mary's Army Auxiliary Corps, collated the official reports on the Auxiliary Territorial Service and left a mass of information in draft form with the Women's Royal Army Corps.

Second, I must thank the staff of the Ministry of Defence (Army) Library and in particular Mr C. H. Potts, who directed my attention to the primary source on which I mainly relied, Miss Stephanie Glover and Miss Erica Watson in the Library of the Royal United Services Institute. Major R. St G. Bartelot, librarian of the Royal Artillery Institution put me in touch with Lieutenant-Colonel J. W. Naylor, late RA, who provided me with a wealth of information about the mixed batteries in Anti-Aircraft Command.

Of the many relevant published works I found four invaluable and I am grateful for the permission given by Hutchinson and Co and Macmillan and Co to quote the short extracts appearing in these pages. They are *Service with the Army*, by Dame Helen Gwynne-Vaughan, *As Thoughts Survive* by Dame Leslie Whateley and *F.A.N.Y. Invicta* by Dame Irene Ward, all published by Hutchinson, and *A Heroine in her Time* by Molly Izzard, published by Macmillan.

My task was eased and made enjoyable by the support, encouragement and information provided by the Deputy Controller-Commandant, Colonel Lucy Davies CBE, the Director, Women's Royal Army Corps, Brigadier Eileen Nolan CB, Dame Frances Coulshed DBE TD, Mrs Christian Fraser-Tytler CBE, Miss Catherine McQuistan TD, Dame Mary Railton DBE, Dame Mary Tyrwhitt DBE and Dame Leslie Whateley DBE.

To these names I must add those of my wife and my daughter, Mrs Conrad Natzio, who brought a trained editorial eye to bear on the draft.

To Mrs Jean Walter who skilfully interpreted and typed a much worked preliminary draft I also owe many thanks.

Finally, having made all these grateful acknowledgements, I must say that the responsibility for any imperfections in this work is mine alone.

Shelford Bidwell

Introduction

General Sir Ronald Adam,
GCB, DSO, OBE

I welcome this history of the Women's services to the Army in two world wars. It is a story that needed to be written and the author has succeeded in producing a most interesting account of the work done by the women of Great Britain for the Army—vital work which helped us to victory in both world wars. I had not realized until I read this history of the contribution made by women in the First World War, but this is due to the fact that my service was mostly overseas. I can vividly recall the contribution made by women in the Second World War.

In 1938 I was present, as DCIGS, at a meeting in the War Office called by the Secretary of State for War, Mr Hore Belisha. Among others present were Dame Helen Gwynne-Vaughan and Sir John Brown, then Assistant Director-General of the Territorial Army. After a short discussion the decision to raise the Auxiliary Territorial Service as part of the Territorial Army was taken and it was announced by the BBC on 3 September, 1938. The view of the General Staff at that time was that war with Germany was imminent, so there was little time for formation of the service. The credit for its rapid formation was due to the Director, Dame Helen Gwynne-Vaughan, a born organizer with wide experience from the First World War. She was ably assisted by ex-members of Queen Mary's Army Auxiliary Corps and a number of voluntary women's organizations, including the oldest of all, the FANY.

When I became Adjutant-General in 1941, Dame Helen Gwynne-Vaughan was at least two years past the retiring age of 60. I reluctantly came to the conclusion that it was time a younger officer assumed command, and told the Secretary of State my opinion. Dame Helen retired shortly afterwards, having carried out a magnificent job. The new Director was Jean Knox, who chose as her Assistant Leslie Whateley, and a very good combination they proved. The Director visited all units, while the Assistant Director ran the office. After a struggle with the Treasury we succeeded in getting the Assistant Director made a Chief Controller, equivalent to a Major-General.

The effect of the Director's visits, for she was always immaculately turned out, was to have an immediate effect on the smartness of the ATS. The Director and her Assistant Director paid particular attention to the welfare of the Service, which improved greatly. As a result, when the Markham Committee carried out its enquiry in 1942, the report was not too bad. Unfortunately the strain on the Director proved too great and in 1943 I received a letter from her saying that she must resign through ill health.

She was succeeded as Director by her Assistant, Leslie Whateley, who carried on most successfully until 1946 and proved an admirable Director. All the controllers did well in the commands, but, as the author points out, Controller Chitty in the Middle East and Controller Fraser-Tytler, who commanded the women in AA Command under General Sir Tim Pile, did particularly well. The latter made magnificent use of the women's services in many roles and understood their employment and welfare better than any other commander. It is not generally realized that the strength of the ATS in the Second World War was equal to that of our peacetime army.

There cannot be much wrong with a nation whose women respond in the way the women of Great Britain did to the needs of their country, and perform so well in time of crisis. The decision to retain the women's services, as the Women's Royal Army Corps and as part of the Regular Army, shows the appreciation of the Army for their efforts.

The Women's
Royal Army Corps

Chapter I

Women in a World at War

ON 31 March, 1917, the vanguard of the Women's Army Auxiliary Corps crossed the English Channel and entered the war zone of the British armies in France. It was hardly a dramatic event: the force consisted of 14 cooks and waitresses under a 'unit administrator' to staff an officers' club in Abbeville. All the same, it is a significant and, indeed, a historic date. After two and a half years of war a dent had finally been made in the wall of military prejudice which had so far barred the employment of any females except those in the nursing and medical services, even in the base areas. It was another step on the long and arduous road women had to travel towards emancipation. It is also the date at which the history of the Women's Royal Army Corps begins, although it was to be another 32 years before it was established under its present title as a regular corps of the British army.

The creation of the Women's Auxiliary Corps was a consummation not reached without unremitting struggle. 'I discovered', recalled Dame Helen Gwynne-Vaughan (neé Fraser) of her arrival in France to become Chief Controller, 'that the objection to the employment of women was almost universal'. It was not as if anyone could be in doubt by the end of 1916 that women possessed ability in leadership and management, or that they could do the work of men: in England they were already filling the gaps in industry left by the men who had joined Kitchener's new armies. At the heart of the question was not so much doubt about the ability or the reliability of women, but an unformulated but powerful fear of the consequences of their intrusion in strength into an entity so exclusively and aggressively male as an army in the field. There was also the deeper hostility which had been aroused by the militancy of the campaign for women's suffrage which had been in full blast when war was declared in 1914.

Women's war service can be said to have been the vigorous child of the suffragist movement which was put into suspense 'for the duration'. They were given the vote without any further disturbances in 1918. All the energy of the militants and of the women who were engaged in more orthodox political activity was voluntarily and enthusiastically redirected into the prosecution of the war. Those who remember the outbreak of war in September, 1939, and the mood of the nation – sombre, serious and determined, and with no illusions about what lay ahead – find it difficult to understand the extraordinary combination of war fever and euphoria which took hold of the British in 1914, only to be dissipated finally when the casualties of the Battle of the Somme in 1916 became known and bitterly felt by almost every family in the country. The war intensified the strong natural feminine instinct to do something – anything – to help their men in a time of conflict. Even if there was no room in nursing or the Voluntary Aid Detachments (VAD) or the Red Cross there must be something (they felt) women could do – scrub floors, *anything*? One or two voluntary, non-medical societies existed but the vast potential of women was waiting to be mobilized. It awaited leadership, and this was to emerge, as it happened, not from the militant 'suffragettes' but the calmer, professional wing of the women's movement.

The key to female emancipation was education. It is difficult for us now to understand a society whose upper classes believed that their own daughters, if educated, would somehow lose their 'femininity', and the terrible struggles and traumas endured by the pioneers of the nineteenth century when they tried to break out of the male-spun cocoon which determined that only the moony, vapid or helpless were attractive bargains in the matrimonial market. Helen Fraser when a girl was ticked off for her subject of conversation with a young man at a dinner party: it was *geometry*! Miss Gardiner, who founded a famous girls' school in East Anglia, said it was to be dedicated to the proposition that women were rational beings – a disturbing idea for Victorian England. (Perhaps the Scots can congratulate themselves on the fact that the first two 'chief controllers' of the Women's Army Auxiliary Corps were Alexandra Mary Geddes and Helen Charlotta Isabella Fraser, one a doctor of medicine and the other a university lecturer in botany.)

Education alone, however, was not enough. To make an impression a degree of political skill was essential, for it must be remembered that it was not only the men who could be obstructive: a large majority of women believed in and even jealously preserved their subordinate and specialized position in the rigid structure of Victorian society; laid down, they believed, for ever by some vague natural or even Divine law. As every soldier is taught, one of the maxims for success is the relentless and determined pursuit of the aim, but in all human relationships tact and skill are required to avoid generating avoidable resistance. Collectively the early leadership of the Corps possessed both these valuable qualities and the choice of *suaviter in modo; fortiter in re** for the motto of the present Women's Royal Army Corps is a happy one.

Knowledge and political skill were essential to start the ball rolling, but managerial ability and clearheadedness were required as well to deal with the mass of administrative detail by which a plan is converted from an idea or a piece of paper – all the endless and boring 'A' and 'Q' work – to a military machine whose component parts are living and breathing human beings. Here again the founder members of the Corps were already experienced. They had cut their administrative teeth in public and social work, in committees, in hospitals and in the senior common room. They knew how the 'machine' worked, and also how to work the machine. They were 'ladies', which was important when dealing with the narrowly recruited military establishment of the day where, in the upper echelon of the War Office, everyone tended to know everyone else. To be connected, as the three first controllers were, to the generals by social ties or actual kinship and to 'speak their language' may seem to us now the pure snobbery of an obsolete caste system, but it was very useful and fully exploited. Helen Gwynne-Vaughan was able to remind the Adjutant-General at a

* 'Gentle in manner; resolute in deed.'

crucial interview that she had 'come out' at a ball given by his regiment, the Gordon Highlanders, in Aberdeen in 1896. But that interview took place in February, 1917, when the soldiers had already been convinced by the bloody economics of the Western Front that they had either to employ women in support tasks or drastically reduce the number of combatant units. To keep a correct historical perspective it is necessary to look first at the preparatory work of the previous war years, the tributaries, as it were, which were finally to unite in the main stream of the development of the Corps.

The earlist and most famous of the voluntary bodies was the First Aid Nursing Yeomanry, formed in 1909, with memories of the South African War in which cavalry and mounted riflemen played so prominent a part. The title Yeomanry was borrowed from the Territorials, who still use this traditional term to describe their cavalry units, and it was recruited from ladies who could ride well with the bizarre aim of scouring the battlefield to locate and retrieve the wounded on horseback. Even before the intensity of firepower in modern war became apparent it was perceived that the chances of survival of such equestrian valkyries were poor, and the FANY sensibly converted themselves to a corps of drivers and mechanics for motor ambulances. For one reason and another the British army at first refused to have anything to do with them, but their services were gratefully accepted by the Belgians and the French. They were to maintain a tradition of devotion and efficiency throughout both wars, fusing with the Auxiliary Territorial Service in the second but keeping their separate identity.

As well, the undirected enthusiasm of the first year of the war produced a number of other women's voluntary organizations – the Women's Emergency Corps, the Women's Auxiliary Force, the Women's Volunteer Motor Drivers, the Home Service Corps and the Women's Volunteer Reserve – all of whom addressed themselves to such tasks as they thought might be helpful without any guidance from above or any coordination. The Women's Volunteer Reserve was the most military in bearing and appearance. Its members bought khaki uniforms, assumed military ranks and coaxed or bribed military instructors to come and drill them in their spare time. The 'rank and file' were largely employed in factories and offices and did a great deal of useful and unselfish work in such spare time as they had, early in the morning or late at night. Nothing, however boring or menial, came amiss to them. They scrubbed the floors of military canteens, salvaged waste paper, dug allotments and later, after the air raids had started, provided amateur first aid parties, special constables and special messengers for the GPO. Their 'colonel-in-chief' was the Marchioness of Londonderry, who deplored their exaggerated military bearing, feeling that a women's service should not assume a pose which men would be quick to ridicule, but it is worth noting that when the women's auxiliary services were formed at last many of their best recruits came from the WVR and proved all the more useful for being acquainted with the rudiments of drill and discipline. The WVR gradually faded away, as Lady Londonderry, when given the opportunity of rendering direct assistance to the army in the Home Commands, did not use it as a base but formed a new corps. Nevertheless Women's Volunteer Reserve, misguided or not as some of its attitudes may have been, had made a small but effective reconnaissance into areas where the army could be supported outside purely medical work, and its errors and failings provided useful lessons for a future model.

The next, and decisive, step forward was taken in the field of army catering. Military catering at its best was execrable (and was to remain so until the forming of the Army Catering Corps, and the virtual army catering revolution after World War II), and any hope of improving it was destroyed by the unplanned, unforeseen need to raise six huge new armies. Sufficient men with the right aptitudes could not be found and trained to keep pace with the demands of new units for cooks by the hundred. The rations, by the nutritional standards of the day, were good and plentiful but were either wasted in preparation or so badly cooked that the men threw them away. The Quartermaster-General, Sir John Cowans, was one of the few senior officers who saw that women could be usefully employed in their most traditional role in non-combatant units or establishments, and he asked Lady Londonderry if she could utilize one of her organizations for the task. She decided to form a new corps altogether (rather than build on the one with whose commanders she had had fundamental disagreements) and this was to be the Women's Legion, a civilian organization, managed by volunteers with the workers on the ground, recruited through the Labour Exchanges and paid through the Army Vote. Its object she defined as 'to provide a capable and efficient body of women whose services could be offered to the State as might be required, to take the place of men needed in the firing line or in other capacities'. Lady Londonderry's ultimate aim was to establish three sections – canteen, ambulance and military cookery, but the immediate need was for cooks, and it is the Military Cookery Section which ties in with the history of the Women's Auxiliary Army Corps.

The venture was a great success, primarily because Lady Londonderry had perceived exactly what was wanted and with excellent judgment had picked exactly the right executive to launch it. By the end of 1916 detachments totalling 2,000 cooks and kitchen staff were working in 200 camps in England. They were recruited from domestic cooks, housewives with practical experience, ladies with diplomas in domestic science and untrained volunteers who were, at first, trained in the kitchens. The improvements were not simply a matter of palatability and good cooking; where women were employed the whole standard of domestic economy was improved out of all recognition. What is more, one woman proved able to do the work of just under two men. Everyone was delighed – except the men who were relieved. The euphoria of the first months of the war soon evaporated, certainly among the rank and file (as their cynical and ribald songs reveal) and few men wanted to exchange a safe billet for prospects of death or mutilation in the trenches. The disgruntled soldier-cooks, before they marched out from the great military convalescent depot in Dartford, sabotaged the new gas ovens, so great was their resentment at being replaced, in August 1915, by the Women's Legion. (The same attitude was perhaps even more strong in 1917. A lance-corporal said to an incoming member of the Women's Army Auxiliary Corps as he watched the males who had been relieved setting off to the front, 'You're sending those men to their deaths'.)

The command structure of what was in fact a corps of non-combatant specialists 2,000 strong shows what good minds un-trammelled by preconceived ideas can create. It would be an amusing and also an instructive exercise to see what a modern team of Staff Duties specialists would produce as a suitable War Establishment table: a full colonel, if not a brigadier, at least in command, DAAGs and DAQMGs, staff captains galore, a quarter-master, a chief clerk, a paymaster, and clerks, orderlies and drivers (MT) *ad lib*. The Military Cookery Section should have been theoretically unworkable. The staff was voluntary and unpaid and consisted of two – Miss Lilian Barker, recruited from her post as Principal of the London County Council Women's Institute, who operated from her flat, assisted by her friend, Miss Francis, as secretary, adjutant, paymaster, clerk, quartermaster and facto-tum. The cooks were recruited through the Labour Exchanges and despatched in the required strength as requested by unit com-manders and were paid by the War Department through Miss Francis. Uniforms were procured by the delightfully simple system of ordering them direct from Selfridges and paying by cheque. There were no records checks, no stores, no indents and no audits.

One of Lilian Barker's recruits was Florence Leach (then Mrs Burleigh Leach, later Dame Florence Simpson). There was a natural resentment felt by the professionally qualified women towards society ladies who felt it was fashionable to dirty their elegant fingers with war work, and Lilian Barker was not impressed when – using her own phrase – 'a vision of radiant beauty' shimmered into her office looking for a job and murmuring some-thing about having kept house for her uncle when he was Governor of Gibraltar. She was told politely that the proper place to apply was the Labour Exchange; that, Miss Barker considered, would see her off. Mrs Leach was back with her card in an hour, and a few weeks later was Head Cook at a convalescent camp near Eastbourne. When Miss Barker went down to see how she was getting on she found her on her hands and knees scrubbing the cookhouse floor herself, as half her staff were ill.

The infallible sign of the truly able person is the ability to detect others of the same quality; and it speaks volumes for Dame Lilian Barker, as she became (she was to be famous as the first Woman Commissioner of H.M. Prisons), that when she was asked to take up another important public appointment she named Florence Leach as her successor. The hand-over consisted of her best wishes and a cash balance of £0-13s-4d. Mrs Leach's husband was the Deputy Director of Personal Services, so apart from her own natural intelligence she had at least an insight into the workings of the War Office machine. She soon grasped that the affairs of the cookery section had to be put on something resembling a business-like basis and the status of herself and the individual workers regularized, but she never pressed too hard. She was not only very intelligent, she knew how to use her beauty and charm effectively, if unostentatiously, in advancing the interests of the Women's Legion and, more important, persuading the army to exploit its capability to the full extent. She negotiated the Army Council Instruction which tidied up her position with great tact. (ACI 441 of 1916. The publication of ACIs – now DCIs – is the instrument having the force of a Regulation by which the Army is managed.) As a result, the Women's Legion detachments came to be employed in most units of the 'static chain'. (Only the military hospitals were excepted; they remained the responsibility of the Voluntary Aid Detachments, the doctors sticking firmly to the women they knew. No doubt there was the same jealousy and competition for role as still persists among the combat corps and regiments.) The Legion's cookery instructors visited and advised other military establishments, and a Legion School of Cookery was set up at Dartford where recruits were trained. All this was a remarkable accomplishment for an untrained woman aided by her sister as a volunteer secretary.

The Women's Legion was, in short, one of those remarkable institutions full of anomalies, the despair of external observers, but run by rank amateurs with enormous efficiency. No one thought it odd that its members wore uniform with badges of rank and worked alongside soldiers but were in all respects civilians. (The Legion had a rather high-toned cap-badge, designed by Lady Londonderry, depicting Victory holding a laurel wreath in her hand; immediately to be identified as a frying-pan.) The Women's Legion continued in its apparently ramshackle form until the end of the war, but it was to be overtaken by the remorseless economics of modern warfare. The man-power first flowed away from industry to the new armies, and in the summer and autumn of 1916 the new armies were to be devoured by the Moloch of the Western Front. Only women were left to take their place behind the lines. Some idea of the scale on which they were needed by September, 1916, is given in a pamphlet called *Women's War Work*, published, with copious illustrations, by the Stationery Office for the War Office with an 'Introductory Note' by the Adjutant-General. The Preface begins by explaining that the formation of large armies had made such demands on men of military age 'that it was incumbent on those not engaged in Military Service to maintain the output of articles required for the War and the export trade. It is considered that a more widespread knowledge of the success which has been attained by Women in nearly all branches is most desirable, and will lead to the release of large numbers of men to the colours who have hitherto been considered indispensable. Employers who have met the new conditions with patience and foresight readily admit that the results achieved by the temporary employment of women far exceed their original estimates . . . how much greater must be the scope for such substitution by those employers who have not attempted it from reasons of apprehension or possibly prejudice?' (A question which the Adjutant-General and the Quartermaster-General were about to address to that most 'apprehensive' of employers: their own service.) Some 2,000 occupations were scheduled, and the illustrations show women at work in 75 of them, ranging from the familiar scenes of women making shells and other munitions to heaving materials around in breweries and steelworks. There are even 'land-girls' dressed in unheard of trousers and puttees carting turnips. As well, of course, there were thousands of women employed as clerks and stenographers in the various ministries.

It was not so much that the contribution of women to the war effort was recognized, but that sheer economic necessity had forced it upon the nation. The last obstacle was the 'no entry' sign on the French shore of the English Channel. What brought that down were the grim figures presented as the final reckoning for the Battle of the Somme which had started with such high hopes in July, 1916. The 'butcher's bill' for the Somme was 440,000 and it was clear that this was not final. Yet more and costlier battles must be fought and yet more reinforcements would be required. Either the huge administrative backing (the 'infrastructure', as it is now termed) essential to a modern army had to be drastically pruned, or further inroads made on the industries which nourished the armies in the field, or the numbers of men in combat units had to be radically reduced. There was talk of calling up men in their late 50s, but even this would not be enough. Somehow agreement had to be obtained from the Commander-in-Chief that women could be employed outside the hospital service and a formal, military organization set up acceptable to all concerned in which they could work.

So far the employment of women had been a piecemeal affair, partly the initiative of the Quartermaster-General with a large and important segment well-established under the Director-General of the Medical Services. Now that there was a crisis over manning, the problem was shifted to the Adjutant-General, the adroit and intelligent Sir Nevil Macready, and his Director of Recruiting Brigadier A. C. Geddes (later Sir Auckland Geddes, and brother of Sir Eric, then Director-General of Transportation of the British armies in France and famous, or infamous, for wielding the 'Geddes Axe' after the war). In December Macready asked the Commander-in-Chief (Haig) whether he would be prepared to accept women, in any capacity, in the static chain. Haig agreed, only stipulating that they should be properly organized and operate in groups of not less than twenty each under their own officers. This was in December, 1916, and the extent of the requirements was made clear in a report on the static chain in France made on the orders of the Army Council by a War Office general. He recommended that 12,000 women could be used in such jobs as ambulance drivers, storemen, clerks, checkers, telegraphists, telephonists, postal employees, orderlies, cooks and domestic servants. This figure took no account of the demand in the home base, which was virtually unlimited. The Commander-in-Chief's wishes and General Lawson's report made it quite clear that no sort of *ad hoc*, amateur organization would serve, but a disciplined corps with a proper command structure, regulations and terms of service administered by its own women officers.

Macready at first favoured the militarily tidy solution of a single integrated women's corps for the whole army, but soon found that this would involve the VAD, a multitude of women so far without any military affiliation engaged in recruiting offices and intelligence duties, and also the Women's Legion. As anyone with experience of Whitehall will understand the simple proposal by the soldiers for a corps approximating as closely as possible to the male army in all matters, including pay, to make for ease of administration, raised a whole forest of objections from civil servants; and to increase the fog the only male, or female, in England who had any practical experience of the subject was Mrs Leach. (Dame Rachel Crowdy-Thornhill, then the able commandant of the VAD in France, in fact also favoured integration.)

This sort of thing could have gone on for ever, but the situation was too urgent, and Geddes took a fateful initiative. A third and equally gifted member of his family was his sister Mary, 44 years old, the first woman to graduate in medicine in the University of Edinburgh, now married to Dr Chalmers Watson; a woman of great warmth of character allied to common sense and determination and with some experience of public affairs. In February she accepted the invitation to raise and command what was to be called the Women's Army Auxiliary Corps and work out its conditions of service.

When in London Mrs Watson called on her cousin, Dr Louisa Garrett Anderson (daughter of Elizabeth Garrett Anderson), who, with Dr Flora Murray, was running the military hospital in Endell Street staffed entirely by women, and there she met Helen Gwynne-Vaughan, a formidable and talented woman whose association with the women's services was to span the two world wars. She was the epitome of the 'new woman', a great beauty in her youth and born an aristocrat (which she never forgot, or allowed anyone else to forget) who had broken the shackles of her family to live on her own, attend London University, obtain a degree, win approval from her male colleagues and marry a scientist of promise and 'good family' but with no social pretensions. Now, at 38, she was most unhappily widowed, and although fully occupied as the head of the Department of Botany in Birkbeck College, she was anxious to do some war work and had trained in medical bacteriology with this in mind. She and Mary Chalmers Watson, although so different — the one gay and buoyant and full of charm, the other cold, steely and with an abrupt manner and a set of jaw which was to frighten many a girl, and not a few men either — found themselves immediately on the same net. A word was passed, and in February, 1917, it was decided; she was to be the senior officer overseas under the command of Mary Watson who was to be based in England, while Florence Leach was to become the controller of cooks, recruiting from her own Women's Legion. So by March, 1917, the three great figures who were to mould the Corps were in the centre of the stage.

Chapter II

With the Armies in France

MILITARY historians — and their readership — are largely concerned with grand questions of strategy and the drama of battle. By contrast, administrative problems are tedious and difficult; it has been well said that of all those so ready to debate, say, the victories of Slim and Montgomery, few will know even the name of their principal administrative officers. No one can be in any doubt about the need for good administrative backing for the armies in the field, or the importance of the part played by the women, but it is as well to be quite clear about the environment in which they had to work.

Only sixty years after the Crimea — and the first impulse given by one of the most famous of Englishwomen — the British armies in France were supported by a huge and efficient administrative machine set up from scratch, without which the combat echelons could not have functioned for more than a few months. A great army in the field is like a socialist state — entirely autocractic, with every citizen's role, status and emoluments exactly fixed by decree and providing everything they need: food, clothes, shops, public baths, holiday centres, courts of law, clubs, hospitals, welfare, public transport, churches and schools — over and above food, weapons and a supply of ammunition and reinforcements. Amateurs of military affairs tend to be scornful of such lavish arrangements, but they are all essential to the comfort and therefore the staying-power of a modern, sophisticated army engaged in a prolonged campaign.

Each major formation, the division, the army corps and the army (of which there were five in France) had its own administrative support element, each larger and more elaborate as they increased in size, until an army was virtually self-contained. As well as a left and right boundary which defined the sphere of tactical action each formation had a rear boundary forward of which its adminstrative support and logistic units were located – lines of communication units, grouped under static 'areas' which contained all the apparatus of depots, hospitals, reinforcement camps, signal centres, Royal Flying Corps airfields and so on. The labour force was male, either uniformed and under the same provisions of military law laid down in the Army Act by Parliament as the combatant soldiers in the regiments and brigades, or civilians, some locally recruited, some imported like the Chinese. To provide female reliefs for the men with female officers competent to manage them was straightforward enough; the difficulty was fitting a female task force into this strictly disciplined, all-male, theoretically celibate society.

It might have been thought that the more closely the Women's Army Auxiliary Corps was assimilated into this system and the more amenable it was to a disciplinary code resembling the Army Act and King's Regulations the more reassured the Army would be, but this was not the case. In the first place the run of the mill officers with whom the WAAC would have to work were suspicious and resentful of any alteration to the existing order of things, either military or social. It was not so much the idea of employing women workers that perturbed them as women 'officers', who might hold rank senior to them, require to be saluted, and even give orders, a prospect which offended their strongly-held ideas of the importance of rank and seniority – very dear to that generation – and of the subordinate status of women. This penetrated even into AG 11, the new section of the Adjutant-General's department set up to implement the decision to form the WAAC. Helen Gwynne-Vaughan records that when travelling with the AAG, a Lieutenant-Colonel Leigh-Wood, she asked him in the course of conversation if his wife was interested in the women's service. He replied discouragingly, 'My wife, Mrs Gwynne-Vaughan, is a truly feminine woman'. This attitude was reinforced by the deep distaste felt in the conservative circles from which the senior officers were drawn for the militant feminism which had been so greatly publicized, and also greatly misrepresented, in the years immediately prior to 1914.

In consequence there was considerable departmental infighting, with the soldiers somewhat equivocally desiring a disciplined service on the one hand and refusing to contemplate a purely or even partially military model on the other, and opposed to them Helen Gwynne-Vaughan, who had already assumed a uniform and put up the badges of a Lieutenant-Colonel on a verbal agreement with GHQ in France, while Mary Chalmers Watson, playing a skilful and diplomatic role as the head of the WAAC in England, strove to play down the image of khaki-clad, saluting, stamping women. The two ladies were entirely agreed in principle as to objectives, but differed as to the amount of *suaviter in modo* to be applied in attaining them. Mary Chalmers Watson was practical and pragmatic; Helen Gwynne-Vaughan was, in the words of her sympathetic biographer, emotionally committed by her parentage to the military way of life and to the women's cause by her innermost convictions. 'She longed to be accepted as part of the army; her sense of importance demanded it. Beneath her capable, level-headed exterior seethed a dangerous mixture of idealism, ambition, dedication and frustrated romanticism'. She was in a very strong position, because while all the argument about status was thundering at Army Council level she in France was actually putting the WAAC to work and having to deal with the minor but imperative conundrums of discipline, administrative procedures, and what a masculine army calls 'man-management'. At this she was superb. She read and digested all the military regulations and methods of handling problems, working seventeen hours a day, and found that much as she would have liked to have had guidance from her male colleagues at GHQ it was they who soon came to rely on her for decisions: apart from the question of drawing up regulations and standing orders '. . . the shortage of soldiers' boxes . . . to provide a woman with a receptacle she could lock; action to be taken in case of misconduct; the disposal of sanitary towels, responsibility of the cleanliness of earth closets, the provision of canteen facilities, physical recreation and social intercourse between the sexes'.

Fortunately she found two able and extremely helpful colleagues in the Adjutant-General's department, Colonel J. B. Wroughton and Lieutenant-Colonel Whitehead. As well she had the loyal support of her Chief Controller in England and, unknown to her at the time, of the Adjutant-General, Macready, but the time was not politically ripe to 'militarize' women, the term including such brash assumptions of masculinity as saying 'sir' when speaking to senior officers and standing up or to attenton when spoken to by them. The Secretary of State had decided that the WAAC was to to be a purely civilian service. This was made known by Macready at GHQ at Montreuil in what amounted to a carpeting of Helen Gwynne-Vaughan. On 21 April, after the deployment of the WAAC was only a month old, she was firmly told that the status of the corps was immutably civilian, the term 'officer' was not to be used, only 'official', saluting (a rather feeble compromise) was was optional, badges of rank would be allowed but there would be no definition of equivalance of rank with the army, and that the only paragraph of King's Regulations applicable to the women's service was that decreeing that orders would be interpreted 'reasonably and intelligently'.

As is often the case in such affairs, in the end a satisfactory if not ideal solution was arrived at, and Helen Gwynne-Vaughan proved fully capable of outmanœuvering the War Office. After all, she was equal or superior in intelligence to the majority of the men she was working with, and had won over those who counted in GHQ. With the help of the AG's branch and the Judge Advocate General she and Colonel Wroughton drafted a set of regulations for the WAAC *in France* which were issued as by the great Field-Marshal Commanding-in-Chief himself over his principal staff officer's signature which the War Office were unlikely to overrule, and they stood, to be confirmed in virtually all respects when the Army Council Instruction (ACI 1069 of July, 1917) was published. Thus she deftly obtained her own way in most of what mattered.

Briefly the structure then was that there were two heads, each

1 *Helen Fraser, later Dame Helen Gwynne-Vaughan, in 1909 –
from the painting by Philip de László*

2   Members of the QMAAC outside their Nissen hut, Rouen, 18 June, 1918

3   QMAAC working in the engine repair shops at Pont de l'Arche

with the rank of 'Chief Controller', the one in France being subordinate to Chief Controller Chalmers Watson at the War Office. (Helen Gwynne-Vaughan characteristically and tersely rejected the title 'Chief Woman Controller', saying that this would abbreviate inevitably into 'Chief WC'.) The two Chief Controllers addressed each other in correspondence puntiliously as 'My Dear CC' and this formality extended down the hierarchy. Below there were 'controllers' in areas and in commands at home, and below them deputy administrators, assistant administrators, administrators, forewomen and assistant forewomen corresponding to NCOs. Badges of rank were combinations of roses and fleurs-de-lis. The officers wore a khaki coat and skirt and the forewomen and 'rank and file', who seemed to have had no official designation and were referred to simply as 'women', (sometimes 'workers') wore a coat-frock, or overalls at work. (There were considerable arguments over details of dress, exactly as in male regiments, but the unforeseen consequence of a piffling War Office ruling that the women were not to use the belts issued with their waterproofs was that it made them resemble maternity garments and so exposed the wearers to jibes. It was eventually rescinded.)

The difficulties over enforcing discipline arose because of the Corps' civilian status and because it was split between the home forces and the armies in France. It must be borne in mind that although public attention was naturally directed towards the WAAC contingent of about 9,000 women in the actual theatre of war, at home there were 29,000 women equally valuably employed. The home contingent was brought under the provisions of the Defence of the Realm Act and could be arraigned before the civil courts for absenteeism or desertion, and the officials were empowered by the terms of enrolment to award minor punishments of which the most severe was a fine of 7s 6d. (37½p). In France, following the army pattern, summary justice was at first the responsibility of male field officers who could award the fines, but they much disliked the task. Under Section 184 of the Army Act camp followers, i.e. women, could be court-martialled for conduct endangering the army, but between this and a small fine or stoppage

3

of leave there was no means of dealing with a delinquent other than sending her home for trial by the civil courts, and it was only for the fourth detected offence that this could be done. Eventually discipline became the responsibility of the theatre Chief Controller and the deputy controllers, and the standing orders drawn up in France came to resemble the orderly room procedures for soldiers which, the modern reader will be interested to learn, both sexes regarded as eminently fair; the women were in favour of having the same code as their male colleagues.

However, it was not the disciplinary code but excellent personnel management by the 'officials' and 'forewomen'—in fact if not in name the 'officers' and 'NCOs'—which produced a Corps whose behaviour, measured statistically, was almost irreproachable, and whose morale was invariably high, bar a few undesirables who inevitably slipped through the recruiting procedures. All the boring but essential domestic economy that goes to make a good unit was learnt and quickly put into action: 'there were regular inspections of accommodation, bath lists and books were compared, mess huts examined, rations and laundry checked, letters censored, dinners and cookhouses inspected, dripping accounts checked, swill bins, boilers, pots and pans carefully scrutinized.' The women were accommodated in camps, self-contained for all purposes, including a sick bay, supervised by medical 'officials' who through the chief woman medical officer, Dr Laura Sandeman, came under the Director-General Army Medical Services. Suitable 'ablutions' were provided, as well as a recreation hut and a YWCA hut. The women were encouraged to make their bleak quarters as homely as possible, with gay curtains, pictures and flowers, and so avoid the depression of spirit felt when after a long day's work the only place to go was a drab barrack hut. They were encouraged to play hockey, cricket and tennis, and organized dances and amateur theatricals.

In June, 1917, when the overseas contingent was already hard at work and growing in strength the Chief Controller, War Office, as Mrs Chalmers Watson was now styled, and Mrs Leach, Controller of Cookery, made a visit of inspection and it did not start well. Chief Controller Gwynne-Vaughan (Mrs Waac, as her male colleagues called her), was fiercely jealous of her command, assertive by nature and had been working for seventeen hours a day for over two months. There had been a divergence of view between the two Chief Controllers, aggravated by the fact that each was under a misapprehension of what the view of the other actually was. Mary Chalmers Watson was naturally sensitive to public feeling about over-militarization of women, while Helen Gwynne-Vaughan felt that her chief did not understand how far the conditions in a theatre of war differed from those at home. Helen, looking back a quarter of a century later recalled of that critical visit that she felt Mrs Chalmers Watson was expecting 'bad organization and some sort of military display'. The early discussions were far from smooth and she said in her usual blunt way that if the War Office was dissatisfied she was prepared to resign.

Mary Chalmers Watson was far too perceptive and sympathetic to be distracted by any of this: she had taken her colleague's measure correctly long before, and perceived that she was over-worked, isolated and consequently under strain. As her visits and discussions proceeded she saw the extent of Helen's achievement. She had established a good relationship with GHQ, the camps were well organized, the women were happy and, best of all, the commanders of units where women were working were full of praise for them. When the Chief Controller returned to London she wrote a generous letter of praise and so harmony, only briefly threatened, was restored.

Mary Chalmers Watson also perceived that what the dynamic and sometimes overbearing Helen Gwynne-Vaughan needed was a confidante and a candid friend, such a relationship as exists in the army between a chief of staff and his commander, or a second-in-command and his CO. In a flash of inspiration she persuaded Helen's sister Marjorie (Mrs Pratt-Barlow) to join the WAAC and posted her to France, where she eventually became an area controller. She, always outwardly correct and using the formal 'ma'am' adopted by the Corps in place of the military 'sir', was able in private to explain to the Chief Controller when her orders or her attitude were causing difficulty. As their mother remarked when she heard of the arrangement, 'At least Marjorie can tell her when to get off her high horse and not to be an ass'. Fortunate indeed is the commander who has such a candid but loyal supporter.

The great Chief Controller's saving was that she had a strong sense of humour, masked though it was by her abrupt and authoritative manner, and she could laugh at herself. She herself recalls in her memoirs how in the course of a discussion she snapped out a demand for more tea. 'We say "Please" in this unit, ma'am', said her sister sweetly. Her ripostes were deadly. A senior staff officer in France at a conference remarked that before the WAAC arrived in France it would be necessary 'to wire in all the woods' to prevent indiscriminate fornication with soldiers (a fear that obsessed both soldiers and civilians at that time). Instead of taking umbrage at what was, however humorously intended, an insulting suggestion, or appearing shocked, she shut him up by observing calmly that if her knowledge of human nature was any guide this would simply present a challenge to all the more determined or enterprising couples. (A rather different answer was given twenty-three odd years later by the ATS officer who came to establish the ATS company deployed at the School of Artillery, Larkhill. Their group of huts had been wired in, and she was teasingly asked if she realized that she was responsible for the morals of her girls, who were surrounded by 'thousands of sex-starved Gunners'. 'Oh yes', she replied, quite unruffled, 'but . . . *quis custodiet* . . . ?')

All the same, Helen Gwynne-Vaughan was feared; not that this was a bad thing. No one has achieved much in the military world without a certain steeliness of character. She impressed on initially reluctant employers that her women were not only reliable and disciplined but 'steady' – the well chosen motto of the WAAC – and not given to what was later called 'flap'. Internally the disciplinary code must be fair, and comparable to the men's, for the men were very conscious of their 'rights' and soon pointed out to the women what their rights were if they thought them to be infringed. Discipline had to be shifted from the mistress-servant girl relationship characteristic of the Victorian era to a concept based on the definition of a 'lawful command' and a code understandable by all, laying down both obligations and rights. Without in any way diminishing the stature of her colleagues it was Helen who saw clearly what was necessary and by her efforts in those few short months between March and May laid the bedrock of discipline and morale on which the women's service was to build, culminating in the present regular Corps.

While all these essential 'A' matters were being unravelled – and the foregoing is only a sketch of what was a very complex affair – the force overseas was being rapidly expanded, and in many places the women were already at work, such as in Records in Rouen, even before the WAAC camps were built and organized. The first expansion was into the Base and Lines of Communication establishments as planned: the Command Paymaster's office at Wimereux, the camp of the Director-General of Transportation, the Royal Air Force Reinforcement Park at Pont de l'Arche, at GHQ itself at Montreuil, and the Tank Reinforcement Park at Le Tréport. Opportunities for fresh work increased as the value of the WAAC became apparent; the army rear boundaries were crossed and by the end of the war clerks, cooks and waitresses were serving in the schools of instruction each had set up in its rear area. Some women worked in the docks supervising the unloading and checking of stores at the very beginning of the Lines of Communication, while the most forward detachments were with Army Signals at St Omer or at Aire with the Royal Enginners. In 1917 a forward office of the Ordnance Survey was moved to France and its female workers accordingly enrolled in the WAAC, suitably kitted and taught drill. (Their instructor, a Sapper sergeant, invariably began with 'Now ladies, will you fall in please?') A small and select party of six assistant administrators, all fluent German speakers, was recruited into the army intelligence radio intercept service for translation and deciphering duties, where they worked long hours and, until May, 1918, without a day off.

Indeed, the hours worked by all the WAAC were staggering, even for wartime, and the way the effort was sustained and morale kept high is a tribute to the leadership of the Corps at all levels.

It is disappointing that little human detail survives from those times; all we have is a roll of names and appointments, but at least these and their services can be briefly and honourably recorded here. Mrs Long, Mrs Leach's sister, who started as her factotum when they took over the Women's Legion cookery section, became Deputy Chief Controller in London when Mrs Leach took over as Chief Controller, after Mrs Chalmers Watson resigned in January for family reasons. Mrs Long, sadly, was killed when the ship she was travelling in was torpedoed in the Channel. Mrs E. H. Pratt became the Deputy Chief Controller in France. Miss Lila Davy transferred from the VAD, with Miss Clowes and Miss Nicholls, and became Chief Controller in France after Mrs Gwynne-Vaughan. The first unit administrator in the field was Miss Frood (later Chief Commander, ATS), who organized the first big camp for staffing the Advanced Mechanical Transport Depot. Miss Carpenter ran the RFC unit at Pont de l'Arche. Miss Penrose was commended for steadiness under shell fire in the crisis of spring, 1918, when she persuaded a number of locally engaged workers to stay at their posts by her example. Mrs Johnson won golden opinions from her commandants in the First Army area, where the WAAC detachments were asked to wear the army sign and the officials to join the mess. Later, when the United States army arrived in France they especially requested the service of a detachment of the WAAC 1,000 strong, commanded at first by Miss Hilda Horniblow as Chief Controller.

By the end of 1917 the WAAC had fully proved itself both at home and in the more difficult environment of France. Mrs Chalmers Watson had been made a Companion of the British Empire (civil in 1917) and in the New Year's Honours List of 1918 Mrs Leach was made CBE (civil) and Mrs Gwynne-Vaughan CBE (military, and the first woman admitted to that division). Then, at this moment of achievement, the WAAC in France became the target of a campaign of slander. It was, perhaps, the inevitable result of a venture so novel, even revolutionary, in an era in which society suffered from sexual constraints and taboos which seem archaic to us today. Mere proximity, it was firmly believed, made sexual intercourse inevitable. Even to be left alone with a man for an hour was dangerous, for longer was to be 'compromised'. Home armies (as opposed to fighting armies, who are too busy trying to stay alive) are hotbeds of rumour, and the stories of misbehaviour, all entirely untrue, were seized on and magnified. Some were picked up and used by German propaganda agents, although why this should have been necessary with the British doing their work for them does not seem clear. The Press as a whole seems to have been fair, reporting the rumours and pouring the cold water of common sense on them. 'Joining the WAAC', commented the *Daily Sketch*, 'isn't either like taking the veil or starting on a career of unbounded skylarking. Army men and Army girls meet on ordinary ground and are friends as girls and men are friends in civil life'. Not that such common-sense views were to prevail. No protests by the Minister of Labour or even the Archbishop of Canterbury who had visited the WAAC in France in July, 1917, had any effect. Nothing is more popular than a shocking and salacious rumour, and salacious the rumours were. The whole scheme of women in military service had been a failure; hundreds of women had been shipped home to give birth to illegitimate children; a soldier (never identified) asserted that he had been on guard duty outside a WAAC Maternity Home. Worse, the WAAC was a cover-plan for a system of army brothels, and the Chief Controller in London, now Mrs Leach, who had been Director of Personnel and Recruiting, had to sign an affidavit that no recruiting for prostitution had ever taken place ('requisitioned or sent to France for any immoral purpose whatever'). The ladies in England were only too ready to believe ill of their serving sisters in France – or in England.

The rumours were only finally squashed when a committee of five worthy ladies were sent out ot investigate. The Adjutant-General at GHQ gravely read out to them a joke from the *Sporting Life*: 'Would you rather have a slap in the eye or a WAAC on the knee?' adding that 'It is the sort of thing we rely on you to prevent'. 'Is there any more?' asked one of the committee hopefully, much to Helen Gwynne-Vaughan's amusement. The committee, after a thorough investigation reported that they found 'a healthy, cheerful, self-respecting body of women, conscious of their position as links in the great chain of the Nation's purpose and zealous in its service'. So the WAAC's good name was cleared.

Apart from the fact that the waking hours of the Corps were almost entirely taken up in work, the leisure time and behaviour of the women and their relationships with men and where they might go when off duty were regulated in a manner that would never be tolerated now: the dangers of rumour had been seen in advance. As against this in the bases the women were permitted, even encouraged, to ask their men friends to the dances they organized, to play tennis and hockey with them, take part in unit sports and meet their friends in approved YMCA or YWCA huts (opened to both sexes after some hesitation). The WAAC became very popular. The social effects were slow to be felt but profound, for it was in France that a large number of young men and women came to work and play together in an unconstrained and natural manner.

There was, of course, the problem of pregnancy, which was then always spoken of in public by metaphor and in hushed voices. Fortunately, careful records had been kept of all reversions to home establishment: 14 for inefficiency, 23 for lack of discipline, one a troublesome case of a professional prostitute who apparently joined with the firm intention of pursuing her trade and was caught, not without trouble, the four ordained times before compulsory reversion to the home establishment was allowed by the tiresome standing orders imposed by the War Office, and 15 pregnant on arrival. A number of married women became pregnant as the natural result of joint leave (carefully noted on the papers in each case). Of illegitimate births the figure recorded was under three per thousand, which was considerably less than for a comparable group in civil life. However, the whole spurious agitation about the morals of the Corps was killed by the visiting committee's report, and anyone who was rash enough to revive it risked a heavy fine under the Defence of the Realm Act. Fortunately public opinion was soon to be distracted by a real crisis.

On 21 March, 1918, a date never to be forgotten, the Germans launched a desperate and, as it turned out, hopeless offensive whose object was to wreck the Franco–British defences from Rheims to Nieuport on the Channel, and to alarmed observers in England it looked for a time as if it was likely to succeed; but then, of course, the further back one is from the front on such occasions the worse things look.

The 'front' – the two rival systems of defence in depth – had been virtually static for two long years, only altering a few miles here and there after immense and costly efforts. In the British sector the base line was the Channel coast from the Somme estuary to Cap Gris Nez running north and south and parallel to the front which was nowhere more than 50–60 miles away as the crow flies. Into this was crammed the whole of the British logistic machine, and if the front was broken it had nowhere to go except across the Channel. On 21 March the Germans opened in the south with Operation 'Michael', driving the over-extended Fifth Army back 45 miles and the Third 25 miles, exposing the right flank of the First. Then 'Georgette' opened on 9 April against the British First and Second Armies and made a bulge in the line which, had it not been sealed off, threatened to cut the British sector in two. It was on 12 April that Haig issued his famous 'backs to the wall' order of the day, but fortunately 'Georgette' petered out on the 11th and 'Blucher-Yorke' was launched in May across the Chemin des Dames against the French Sixth Army who held it, although at its deepest penetration the Germans came within 35 miles of Paris.

The 'flap', as can be imagined, was considerable. The army schools were closed down and pupils and staff sent up to their divisions, the contents of the reinforcement camps hastily marched off to the front, leaving a large number of WAAC units unemployed, and the staff began to pull back the more forward static units threatened by the German advance. Aire, where Assistant Administrator Penrose was working in the Royal Engineer North Special Works Park, came under long range shell fire, but in spite of the threat it was with 'horrified regret' that the Chief

Controller learnt that all the women were to be sent back from the signal centre at St Omer. This order was, to her satisfaction, cancelled at the request of the Director of Signals who said that if his 142 women, who had behaved with exemplary calm under air raids, were removed, he would not be responsible for communications between GHQ at Montreuil and HQ Second Army at Cassel, which were vital to the conduct of the battle. 'So ended,' recorded the Chief Controller, 'the only attempt to withdraw members of the Corps from duty for the sake of their own safety'. The proposal, from England, to withdraw the whole WAAC contingent from France fortunately came to nothing.

There remained the problem of redeployment. Helen Gwynne-Vaughan's distinguished biographer has analysed her deep wish to identify with the soldiers and while she was never an Amazon—she was too feminine for that—what a magnificent staff officer she would have made! By 29 March she had obtained a clear idea of the situation, where the static units were going and what women would be spare, and was busy 'phoning around to her area controllers and administrators for estimates of accommodation so that all the various establishments could continue to be manned after the move. On 31 March when things looked very bad she was called to GHQ to be asked what should be done about the women and she was able to produce a complete plan, typed and ready, having anticipated the question as a good staff officer should. Great was the relief when her friend Colonel Whitehead hurried her into the Deputy Adjutant-General's office with the words, 'Look, sir, Mrs Gwynne-Vaughan has got it all worked out!'

The redeployment was achieved after a great deal of bumping about in cattle trucks ('*hommes 40–chevaux 8*') and uncomfortable lorries and one detachment had to march some distance, but was without incident. (There was one lurid story, never confirmed, that the convoy of lorries carrying women from the Fifth Army Infantry School ran the gauntlet of German machine guns and only escaped by driving across country, but as they were moving sideways from St Valéry-sur-Somme to Boulogne it is difficult to believe.) The greatest danger the women were in was from air raids which the Germans were now able to launch from their new forward fields, but the only casualties were at Abbeville, where eight were killed and six wounded sheltering in a trench. The women all behaved admirably and three were decorated with the Military Medal for their efforts to rescue those buried and for giving first aid under fire. Otherwise the Commander-in-Chief refused to commend the WAAC specially for their steadiness or to mention in orders that never once did air raids prevent them from working. This, he said, was normal for soldiers and required no remark, a ruling that the Chief Controller and all ranks felt was exactly what they wanted, and highly gratifying.

So was the statement on 9 April, the day 'Georgette' was launched, that as a mark of appreciation for the 'good services rendered by the Corps both at home and abroad since its inauguration, especially of the distinction it had earned in France by its work for the army during the recent heavy fighting on the Western Front, the Queen was graciously pleased to assume the position and title of "Commandant-in-Chief", and that in future the Corps was to be known as Queen Mary's Army Auxiliary Corps'. This was an excellent title and one cannot but regret that it disappeared. It described the Corps exactly, it contained the Royal element and it could not be abbreviated into some undignified acronym. Everyone was very pleased and on 19 April Queen Mary sent for Mrs Leach and commanded her to convey a message to the women, 'that the Queen was very much interested in the work and welfare of the Corps, is pleased to be its Commandant-in-Chief and wishes it every success'.

There is little more to tell. The Corps became ever more professional, fresh tasks were assumed, the ever active Chief Controller in France started up a Corps School for administrators and forewomen on the model of the army schools and there were the usual minor troubles that occur in any organization. There was a certain amount of what a later army called 'belly-aching': about hospitalization, and details of dress, and from the women who had passed from Mrs Gwynne-Vaughan's régime to Miss Horniblow's in the detachment with the United States Army. (Perversely, and exactly like male soldiers, they preferred the tightly disciplined unit to one more lax: in the former a soldier always knows where he is and how he stands.) Miss Horniblow became a Chief Controller and, to preserve the hierarchy, Mrs Leach became Controller-in-Chief and ranked as a major-general.

There were numerous changes in senior appointments, but the most momentous was the posting of Mrs Gwynne-Vaughan to the newly formed Women's Royal Air Force, where there had been command troubles. She jibbed, and the Adjutant-General rashly asked her, 'You surely don't consider yourself indispensable to the Corps in France?' 'It hadn't occurred to me to consider myself indispensable to the Royal Air Force, sir' she replied. It was always difficult to serve Helen Gwynne-Vaughan a conversational ace. But the great disciplinarian was disciplined herself and went on to perform briefly but brilliantly in a rewarding task, where she found a cadre of 6,000 QMAAC who had been transferred. She was succeeded in France by Lila Davy, selected from a short list she gave the Adjutant-General who had asked her for suggestions about a successor. 'Those who knew her best were not deceived by her rather vague personality, quick smile and gentle voice. She was a woman of striking personality, fearless, disinterested, humble and possessed of a keen sense of humour. All of her life was influenced by her strong religious convictions.' (Unlike Helen Gwynne-Vaughan, scientist and agnostic.)

Demobilization was slow, but by 31 December, 1920, when the war officially ended, nearly all the women had gone home, except for a small unit who remained to assist the War Graves Commission.

'Difficulties, discomfort, and in many cases the dangers of war, have always been faced bravely and cheerfully and the discipline of the Corps throughout is worthy of the highest praise, and has been in accordance with the best traditions of the army', said the Army Council. Kind and generous words, but they did not prevent the final disbandment of the QMAAC on 27 September, 1921, leaving not so much as a cadre on which to reform, were it ever to be needed again. Fortunately when ten years later there was again a demand for a women's service, the skill and loyalty of the earlier Corps had been preserved and a former Chief Controller, now sixty years old but as clear-headed and iron-willed as ever, was ready to take the helm.

Chapter III

Beginning Again

THE abolition of the military side of the women's services was short-sighted, to say the least of it, but it was one of the many wrong decisions of the period which must be judged in their proper historical context. Although we can see now that the war had altered Britain's social structure and the position of women profoundly, this was by no means plainly visible or widely recognized at the time: the mood was to return to the safe normality of pre-1914. The armed forces were no exception. The military lessons of the war were in fact deeply studied and many sound conclusions emerged, but they were pigeon-holed and sometimes even suppressed. The military history of the inter-war period is one of a long drawn-out battle between the reformers and the dull minds and dead hands of the old guard on whom the responsibility for planning future defence had fallen. The excuses were the economic plight of the country, a direct result of the war, and that the war in the trenches had been a unique disaster unlikely to recur, but the real motive was to return to an army uncontaminated by intellect or machinery and adapted solely for the duties of peace and imperial military policing. In the struggles to abolish the horse and with it the vast mass of useless and decorative cavalry (the social symbol of the desirable but forever lost past), to mechanize and re-equip the artillery, modernize the infantry, establish army aviation and create a tank arm the cause of the women was merely a lost skirmish. Fortunately its leaders, temporarily defeated, took to guerrilla warfare of a type for which they had a natural aptitude – the voluntary association, the committee, the pressure group and the luncheon table – and after many vicissitudes victory came with the re-birth, under the non-committal title of the Auxiliary Territorial Service, in 1938.

With the other social changes the Great War marked the breakthrough of the women's cause on every level, but the struggle was by no means over. In March, 1919, the War Department promised that the QMAAC would remain in some form on a regular basis, and oddly enough this produced quite a hostile reaction in the Press. One paper quoted an unidentified general who was reported as saying that he thought the proposal was 'unthinkable' and 'humorous', voicing the old fears that if men and women mixed it would be 'the destruction of discipline' and the reaction of soldiers' wives if 'unmarried women were allowed to enter freely all the barrack rooms' (an entirely imaginary state of affairs) — indicative of the subconscious fear and resentment of women which persisted among the deeply conservative senior ranks. Inevitably that horse never ran.

A practical and cheap idea which would have commanded strong support from the women was to use the machinery of the Territorial Army, then being reconstituted after the war. The Territorial Army in peace was managed in all respects except military organization and training by the County Associations, the boundaries of responsibility being finely drawn. In the War Office there was a Director-General of the Territorial Army who, later, in the crucial period 1938–39, was to be assisted by a Deputy Director-General, Sir John Brown, who was a Territorial officer. At unit level in peacetime the only regular officer was the adjutant, assisted by a small permanent staff, who served a part-time, volunteer commanding officer and upon whom the whole burden of administration, training and preparations for mobilization involving a complex and detailed plan fell in practice. On mobilization the Territorial units and formations were 'embodied', shedding their 'territorial' status and becoming regular army units under the War Department in every respect, and the Associations ceased to have any responsibility and went into suspended animation for the duration of the war.

The War Office plan was based on the assumption that in a

general war the services of women would be essential, and that the officers must be commissioned and the rank and file enlisted, thus bringing them under the Army Act and avoiding the half-baked enrolment procedures, neither wholly civilian nor wholly unmilitary and easily made unworkable by anyone who chose to disobey orders or regulations. In peacetime a cadre of suitably trained women, to be called 'the Queen's Reserve', was to form part of the Territorial forces. This was far-sighted and indeed what eventually through force of circumstances was to come about, but in the early 1920s the climate of opinion was not right and the energies of the women's leaders had been attracted to other causes, or, like Mrs Chalmers Watson and Dame Florence Simpson (as Mrs Leach became), they had retired into private life. The scheme was pigeon-holed.

There remained in being two independent, voluntary associations, or societies, to which can be added the QMAAC Old Comrades Association which was an effective reservoir of capable women and a lobby which, through its appearance on such occasions as Remembrance Day, kept the idea of women's military service alive. Lady Londonderry's Women's Legion had been largely dissipated or absorbed by the WAAC and later the WRAF, but its Motor Transport Section had remained in being for service at home and after the war it reconstituted itself as a voluntary society under the Women's Legion title. It rallied to the government in the General Strike of 1926, and had been recognized by the War Office as a voluntary body ready to assist the army if called upon.

The First Aid Nursing Yeomanry—subtitled the Ambulance Car Corps and later officially the Women's Transport Service, but inevitably and forever FANY, with a short 'a'—had a strong sense of achievement, a powerful *esprit de corps* and, after their experiences of 1914–16, when their services had been coldly rejected by their own army, had no particular sense of obligation to the establishment and intended to remain autonomous and independent, cooperating only on their own terms. FANY was run not by dilettantes but by practical women, administering its affairs efficiently through a

4 & 5   *Cooking for the troops 1918–1975*

6 *HM Queen Mary inspects her own Corps at Aldershot in 1918*

7 *HM The Queen Mother talking to the cooks at Liphook*

paid commandant responsible to an advisory committee. They perceived that it would not be sensible to compete with the already fully subscribed nursing and voluntary bodies but to concentrate on army transport – ambulances and later other forms of wheeled vehicles suitable for women drivers. They affiliated themselves to the Royal Army Service Corps (now the Royal Corps of Transport) and invited a distinguished former member of that Corps, General Sir Evan Gibb, to be their honorary colonel and adviser.

In 1921 the FANY restarted serious peacetime training, holding annual camps, with tents and equipment wheedled out of the Brigade of Guards, and instructors invited from appropriate regular units. Like the Women's Legion, the FANY turned out in strength in 1926 and were awarded recognition in Army Order 94 of 31 March, 1927, which contained the cautious proviso that 'the corps will receive no assistance from army funds', but this strengthened their hands as regards material assistance and gained them admission to courses at the School of Mechanical Transport and, as anti-gas training was seen to be a necessary part of military training, at the School of Chemical Warfare at Winterbourne Gunner.

The FANY's strength was that it was recruited very largely from upper middle and upper-class girls, unemployed because their rigid social conventions barred them from all but a few jobs or professions. (Strange as this may seem at so late a date, it was so. The present writer well remembers the ripple of dismay which ran through the wives of a certain regiment – not his own – when it was learnt that the otherwise acceptable young lady who had become engaged to one of 'their' subalterns had *worked in a shop*.) Such girls were longing for useful work to do, had the time to give and the necessary education to absorb training and the resultant standard of achievement was very high. The subjects included army administration, unit management, drill and discipline, as well as hygiene, anti-gas precautions, driving, convoy drills, motor mechanics and repairs, radio communication procedures and switchboard operating. The FANY, in fact, resembled in some respects the Honourable Artillery Company, its ranks filled with

4

officer material and its morale reinforced by the sense of belonging to a common class as well as having a common, patriotic aim. In consequence not only were they jealous of their independence from officialdom but of any hint that they might surrender part of it to any enlarged women's service that might be formed.

So the matter rested until 1934, when the signs of an approaching European crisis became visible to those who chose to notice and interpret them and the War Department was sufficiently perturbed to be interested once more in laying down at least the basis of a women's service ready to mobilize in the event of war. The initiative was taken by Lady Londonderry, the creator of the Women's Legion. Circe Londonderry, wife of the Secretary of State for Air, *grande dame*, famous both as a society and political hostess, was looked at askance by the professional women who had reached their own positions the hard way, as a moneyed, aristocratic amateur, but she was determined, clever, highly influential, politically astute and impelled by a strong sense of public duty. What she needed was a strong committee, and it was inevitable that she should have turned to Helen Gwynne-Vaughan.

The former lecturer in botany had by this time emerged as great a lady as Lady Londonderry. After leaving QMAAC she had made a success of her tour in command of the Women's Royal Air Force which rapidly recovered under her direction from its former leadership troubles, she had been made a Dame, later to be raised to Dame Grand Cross, of the Order of the British Empire, she had been awarded the Traill Medal of the Linnaean Society, she was now a professor of the University of London and had been elected to the Senate of that University as one of the representatives of the faculty of science. After the failure of three determined efforts to be elected to Parliament she had turned to that side of public life where the voluntary services of gifted people who are prepared to sit on valuable but tedious and boring committees is especially welcome. She had never amid all these concerns neglected her goal of service for women in support of the armed forces, and kept her link with the veterans of France through her vice-presidency of the QMAAC Old Comrades Association and the WRAF.

She was determined to be in on any political activity towards that end and, no doubt, from the first was equally determined, if ever a chief executive was required, to secure the post for herself, for she was supremely confident in her own ability. Lady Londonderry's position was not dependent on what the Duke of Wellington called any 'damned merit': hers, for all her Fraser and Fergusson ancestry, was owed entirely to merit. The two ladies were very different in character and approach and were not always in sympathy. They could have been, destructively, rivals, but happily they made a formidable alliance.

The campaign for the creation of a women's service was long, its manoeuvres involved, and it was fought in many a committee and conference and with many a telephone call and at many a luncheon and dinner table. To shorten and simplify a complicated story, Lady Londonderry's idea was to recreate the Women's Legion and bring into it the VADs, the surviving Motor Transport Section of the old Legion and the FANY. Nothing came of this, for one reason and another, except for the creation of the Emergency Service, which started off as the Officer Training Section of the 'new' Women's Legion, which never materialized, and then turned itself into a voluntary society with the Duchess of Gloucester as president and with the blessing of the Army and the RAF. (For a long time, until the decision to form the separate WAAF, the intention was to create a corps able to support either service; the Royal Navy inevitably managed its own affairs in its own way and independently.)

Dame Helen had seen in her usual clear-headed way that the key to successful expansion was the provision of an adequate number of properly trained officers; not technically trained but what the male army calls 'regimental' soldiers, who provide the leadership and personnel management and are well grounded in all questions of office routine, law, administration, discipline and the welfare of the rank and file. True, the only finishing school is practice in a unit already staffed with good NCOs, but to begin, uninstructed, all ranks together, without the faintest notion of how to move a party from one location to another, give an order or obtain a military store is a recipe for chaos. (As had been unnecessarily discovered in Kitchener's New Armies, and was to be even more unnecessarily re-discovered in the Auxiliary Territorial Service in 1939.) Emergency Service during its short life was extremely successful and helped to mitigate this state of affairs and provided many excellent officers, including Jean Trefusis Forbes, a professional woman who ran a large kennels and who was to become the Director of the WAAF. It recruited its 'cadets', rather like the FANY, on a friendship basis from educated women, whose relatives thought them eccentric if not actually subversive because of their strange addiction to military training. Instruction was along the proved army style of learning by doing. At camp the class formed its own units, administering itself, cooking for itself, doing all the domestic chores, and rotating appointments so as to obtain experience in every rank. There were 'TEWTS', imaginary exercises without troops where typical situations were given as questions and the students had to offer solutions. As well as lectures, drill and physical training it involved hard living, the beds being uncomfortable, the rooms cold and the food execrable; the cooks of the day on one occasion boiling a Royal Signals brassard in the rice, turning it blue, which was fortunately mistaken for a gastronomic refinement.

In 1936, therefore, things, though moving slowly, looked promising, but in mid-1937 a disappointing, and undoubtedly ill-considered, decision on the part of the Cabinet was conveyed to each of the societies through the Adjutant-General. This was that the whole idea of a women's service had been discarded and that if war broke out the necessary women would be recruited through the Ministry of Labour as civilians. That was in August. In December, just after a new Adjutant-General had taken over (Lieutenant-General Sir Clive Liddell) he sent for Dame Helen and in the presence of his Director of Recruiting told her that the decision was to be shortly officially reversed, and that 17,000 women would be required as a start on mobilization and – inevitably! – yet another advisory council was to be set up, of which Dame Helen was to be a member. This was an interesting *volte face* because neither

Adjutant-Generals nor cabinets act unbriefed and it may be that someone lower in the pile had seized the opportunity of change of incumbent to slip in a fresh appreciation. The result was another scheme for amalgamation. The FANY was to come in *en bloc*, with the aim of providing a core of trained women and potential officers. Emergency Training would turn itself into a permanent officer training school and the Women's Legion would recruit the trades: 600 drivers, 1,800 clerks and 3,600 domestics. Miss Baxter Ellis, Commandant of FANY, who afterwards averred that she never understood the scheme properly, was offered the overall command or directorship, but after consultation with Sir Evan Gibb, on behalf of her Council, withdrew. As a result the whole project was abandoned, to the chagrin of Lady Londonderry.

By then it was the Spring of 1938, the year of the Sudetenland crisis and 'Munich'. Something approaching a sense of urgency was felt in Whitehall and a new scheme propounded, in which the voluntary societies were to be united inside the framework of the Territorial Army, although they would not be of it. (Commissioning of officers, enlistment of women and a disciplinary organization identical with the military were to stick in military throats until 1941.) The Advisory Council was now to contain some heavy-weights, the Parliamentary Under-Secretary – normally responsible for Territorial Affairs, the Deputy Director-General TA – the only Territorial Major-General, Sir John Brown, the Territorial Army Associations, through their permanent, professional secretaries – usually retired officers – and the representatives of the voluntary societies. The FANY agreed to participate only if conditions guaranteeing their identity and independence were met, but the time for bargaining had run out. They were told to agree, or be omitted, and joined under duress, only partially reassured by a gentleman's agreement that their feelings would be respected, obtained from Sir John Brown by Sir Evan Gibb. The scheme had to be pushed through with speed because, apart from the obvious military requirement, opinion in the country was in advance of that at Whitehall, certainly as far as the women were concerned, and many good potential recruits were turning to other forms of voluntary service and new, inexperienced voluntary bodies were appearing like mushrooms. Even before a reply from the FANY had been received the Auxiliary Territorial Service was brought officially into existence by Royal Warrant on 9 September, 1938. In the formal language of such important documents:

'George R.I.
Whereas we deem it expedient to provide an organization whereby certain non-combatant duties in connection with our military and air forces may from time to time be performed by women:
Our will and pleasure is that there shall be formed an organization to be designated the Auxiliary Territorial Service . . .'

(It will be noted that originally the plan was for the ATS to support both the Army and the Royal Air Force. When it was decided that the Royal Air Force should have its own women's service, the Women's Auxiliary Air Force, the ATS companies raised for this purpose were transferred to it.) On 27 September this was made public through the BBC in an announcement after the 9 o'clock evening news.

The inevitable penalty for interminable haverings over principles and administrative details, followed by a panic stricken rush into action without solid preparation, was chaos, and although the year of peace obtained at Munich gave a breathing space in which much good work to produce order was done, its effects were to be felt until 1941. By 28 September the outline of the scheme had been sent to the County Associations, but there had been no time to translate this into the concrete orders for the regular TA adjutants of units, who were immersed in the task of looking over their mobilization and embodiment schemes by way of precaution, when every office was inundated by telephone calls or worse, besieged by women demanding to be enrolled then and there. Hell has no fury like a volunteer scorned, and the best that the wretched officers could do by way of self-defence was to proclaim their ignorance, protest their goodwill and take all the names and addresses and promise to inform the scornful and indignant ladies in due course.

In October, when the dust had settled somewhat, the Service gained a notable recruit. Her Royal Highness the Princess Royal⋆ expressed a desire to join and accepted the honorary appointment of Controller for the West Riding of Yorkshire, to be formally enrolled as a Chief Controller in February, 1940. Her Majesty the Queen (today Queen Elizabeth the Queen Mother) graciously accepted the appointment of Commander-in-Chief shortly after the war broke out in 1939, and in August, 1941, the Princess Royal was gazetted Controller Commandant. All the Royal ladies gave their whole-hearted support to the three women's services, our present Queen joining the ATS when she was old enough and training as a driver. The Princess Royal acted as a wise regimental colonel, keeping herself fully informed of the state of the ATS and its current problems whether they were concerned with organization, clothing or morale, and always offering invaluable advice.

The position before embodiment in 1939 was in outline as follows: The Association appointed female County Commandants who in turn selected officers and through them enrolled women for the companies to be raised in each county. This was most unsatisfactory from the point of view of the FANY, who by virtue of their experience of motor transport and their thorough military training composed almost a hundred per cent of the transport companies from officers to drivers. There was a short and uneasy period of dual control by the County Commandants and the FANY chain of command. This was resolved by re-organizing the motor transport so that the companies were all run by Miss Baxter Ellis from a central HQ in London. The FANY preferred, regardless of any agreements, gentlemen's or otherwise, to go on in their own way for the excellent reason that they felt they knew what they were doing while the newly appointed commandants at that stage of affairs were frankly beginners.

⋆ Princess Mary, daughter of His Majesty King George V and aunt of our present Queen, married to the Earl of Harewood.

The subsequent status of FANY can conveniently be made clear at this point. On 21 September, 1938, after the Royal Warrant establishing the ATS had been published, the Deputy Director General of the Territorial Army held a meeting in the War Office of representatives of the three voluntary organizations – the Motor Transport Service (FANY), the Women's Legion and Emergency Service – to define their commitments to the new service. On behalf of FANY Lady Hailsham and Miss Baxter Ellis signed the agreement and promised to assist the TA Associations to raise 1,500 women in ten companies. Later there were both FANY driver companies and ATS driver companies, but the members of FANY, while being ATS in every military and legal sense, were allowed to retain their identity and designation, wearing a shoulder designation with their title, very much in the same way as the Territorial Yeomanry regiments originally raised as horsed cavalry who were transferred to the Royal Armoured Corps and the Royal Artillery retained their titles. The members of FANY who were completely absorbed into the ATS continued to make the most distinguished contribution to its work, which was, by virtue of their special skills, concentrated on the Motor Transport side, providing commanders, adjutants and instructors for the three Motor Transport Training Centres. Senior Controller Miss Baxter Ellis became Inspector of Motor Companies and also head of MT 10, the section in the training directorate responsible for all ATS training, basic and technical. Sergeant Molly Railton rose to be Director, Women's Royal Army Corps and is now Dame Mary Railton DBE. During the 1939–45 war six were appointed OBE and eight MBE.

Another wing of FANY chose to remain entirely independent, supporting, among other useful activities, the clandestine services. Their exciting history lies outside the scope of this work. In 1942, following a trend to avoid the proliferation of corps and to bring various groups of women under the aegis of the ATS, the Director ATS was offered the option of extending her sphere of activity in that direction, but she advised that, in view of the great expansion of the ATS under way and her attendant organizational problems, her Service should concentrate on its priority task of supporting the Army.

The Officer School of Instruction, based on Emergency Service and run by Dame Helen and her sister, and whose chief instructor was Miss Forbes, was in action without delay, the first course assembling in the Duke of York's HQ on 10 October; but the output never approached the demand. The FANY were self-contained with a built-in supply of officers, but the ATS was to suffer from the complaint common to all the Territorial Army, that too often officers were chosen perforce for availability and willingness without regard for knowledge or potential, tolerable and even valuable in a peacetime service but too often inadequate for full-time employment in war. Many had to be disposed of later which caused much heartburning.

(An anecdote in Dame Helen's *Service with the Army* is revealing. A woman with a good honours degree and business and organizing experience and ready to serve at home or overseas applied for a commission. At her interview the County Commandant said that she did not even know the procedure for applying for commissions and suggested: 'The best place for you would be on the clerical staff. We have classes where you can learn to write letters and fill in forms ... or perhaps you would like to do a little cooking?')

Companies were enrolled as best they could be. There were specialist companies of drivers and clerks (but thoughtlessly unprovided with any general duties women such as cooks) and general duties companies, who formed the majority, consisting of a standard mix of clerks, storewomen, cooks and GD women. Not all units were very clear about their tasks on embodiment, and training directives sent out from the TA Directorate dealt only with basics, it being assumed that enrolment had been by aptitude or civil training. All this should have been a recipe for disaster but enthusiasm and common sense prevailed, and the regular and TA units nearby helped willingly with specialist training.

The most important development was in the higher direction. In May the TA Directorate was thrown into turmoil by the unforeseen decision to double the Territorial Army. At the receiving end in the directorate two male staff officers in TA 5 struggled to deal with every aspect of the command and management of a corps whose ceiling was 17,000 women, from mobilization to military training and discipline to the type of undergarments to be procured and stocked by the ordnance service. It was decided, and not before time, to appoint a full-time female Director ATS, properly assisted by an ATS deputy director and an ATS staff of two other officers. Significantly more than one senior woman, Miss Baxter Ellis of FANY, for example, were opposed to the appointment of a 'head woman', but each of the three services appointed one within a few days of each other. The Secretary of State seems to have had no hesitation in appointing Dame Helen as the only possible and outstanding candidate, and she in turn invited Mrs Christian Fraser Tytler, who had been running an ATS Company in Inverness-shire, to join her as deputy. She took up her duties on 3 July, 1939.

There was an enormous amount to do. All the defects arising from a late start and the shortage of trained officers the new Director had foreseen could not be put right in the two months remaining before the outbreak of war. Although much was achieved, the embodiment and mobilization was what the army calls a 'shambles' and the ATS got off to a bad start through no fault of its own. Nevertheless, the value of the women's service had been recognized, the corps had been once more established and the women were again in their rightful place in support of their country at war.

Chapter IV

Back to Work

In military matters it is sometimes as well not to have too cut-and-dried a plan, too exact a definition of role or charter, too many regulations and standing orders covering every eventuality, for warfare is largely an affair of the unforeseen where a firm grasp of essentials assisted by imagination and initiative are the best guides. This appears to have been the watchword of the ATS on embodiment. All things considered the mobilization of the Territorial Army as a whole went with remarkable smoothness, but there were many astonishing muddles, still the subject of legend and hilarious anecdote. The ATS, a newly created service, its status *vis-à-vis* the army uncertain, its disciplinary code inadequate, its officers with only vestigial training and even its scale of clothing undetermined and its mobilization scheme only half-developed, had its fair share of the muddle. There was undoubtedly hardship, some discontent and resentment which had a lasting effect and rebounded later on the service when the initial excitement of the outbreak of war and deployment to strange new tasks was over. All the same, the record of 1939–40 is one of cutting through muddle, short-circuiting obstructions and magnificently setting to work wherever work was to be done.

A superb example of this spirit was the reaction of Senior Commandant B. Boyle to the unexpected arrival in Thurso, in Caithness, of a contingent of starving troops who were decanted by some destroyers of the Royal Navy after evacuating them from the disastrous campaign in Norway on 1940. Belinda Boyle happened to be visiting her two ATS clerks attached to the little garrison, whose commander was understandably baffled, as whatever he was geared to do it was not suddenly to produce the resources of a transit camp for the debris of a defeated army. Nor was it any use to send them on, for Thurso was a long way from anywhere and the men were starving. The arrival of a horde of fighting men at some tranquil post on the static chain, with dismay on one side and fury and frustration on the other, are the subject of more than one anecdote and things might have been awkward. Senior Commandant Boyle, however, rapidly appreciated the situation and saw that the first priority was food; but from where was she to produce a meal for this ravenous horde? She had a sheaf of billeting forms and, rapidly amending the relevant portions for requisitioning accommodation, requisitioned a flock of sheep, a field of cabbages and some groceries, so securing the basic supplies. For obtaining labour her personality seems to have been sufficient and no forms were needed; the Boy Scouts, called from school, rounded up the sheep, willing butchers slaughtered and jointed them, eleven patriotic housewives and the two ATS clerks made a giant stew in various coppers, buckets and a bath, and the situation was saved.

A Gurkha officer once said to Slim of a raw British battalion, 'Sahib, if you left those men in a field with some sheep and a box of matches they would starve to death.' Clearly the ATS in 1940 were made of sterner and more practical stuff. (It is said that the financial authorities took 'some time' to adjust the matter: connoisseurs of such cases can well believe it: the subsequent correspondence must have been worth reading.)

Such drastic measures were not normally necessary, but a great deal of intelligent adjustment was required on the part of women flung into a military world run by men according to a complicated and dimly understood rule book.

Sometimes, when they encountered a really good unit, they were helped. Junior Commander (Captain) A. Bell, for instance, was attached with her company to a Brigade of Guards training battalion. Predictably, everything had been planned for her arrival and no detail affecting the comfort of the women had been forgotten. She herself was treated as if she was a newly joined ensign, being attached in succession to a company sergeant-major for instruction in office administration, to the Pay Sergeant to learn how to deal with pay and allowances and the Regimental Quartermaster-Sergeant for the mysteries of indenting for stores and the fitting of uniforms. She provides a comical account of being introduced, unbriefed, to that dread ceremony, 'CO's Orders', where she watched, with amazement and with no clear idea of what was happening, guardsmen on charges being marched in and out to the bellowing of sergeant-majors, the clumping of huge glistening boots, the staccato reading of the charge, the evidence and the sentence. Finding that she was too shy to enter the Officers' Mess the Commanding Officer went to fetch her himself, on the first occasion, and arranged in future that, whenever she wanted to dine in Mess, an officer would be sent to escort her. This to us today may seem ridiculously coy, but 37 years ago for a woman, attended or unattended, to enter any part of an Officers' Mess or a men's club except for the special rooms set apart for the purpose was unheard of.

Not all deployments were as smooth or as agreeable as that, for apart from the fact that a great many hastily recruited ATS officers had had no time to discover how the army worked, what they were supposed to do or even how to obtain what they wanted, there were equally a great many male officers, understandably perhaps, in newly-mobilized units barely capable of administering their own troops, let alone a strange sub-unit of women injected into what was already a muddle. In units in which, it can be surmised, the man as well as the woman-management was bad, the ATS were neglected, their officers given no office, their rank and file no canteen facilities or rest room, their 'sub-officers' (as the NCOs were then termed) made to eat with the rank and file and, worst of all, they were starved of work.

All this depended on the nature of the job. Those who suffered worst perhaps were those who when called up had not been fitted into any plan for employment. They helped the territorial adjutants during the flurry of embodiment, turning their hands to whatever was necessary, but the whole TA machinery ceased to exist when this was complete and the unit had left to join its division or brigade in its mobilization area. Some women were left hanging about or moved from pillar to post, not finding a proper home until Christmas. This was very unsettling and helped to fuel the discontent which was to build up in the next eighteen months.

There were no such difficulties in the locally raised and employed companies who fitted smoothly enough into the neighbouring static units such as area headquarters or Pay and Record offices. They lived in billets, or sometimes even in their own homes, going to work daily as if they were civilians and often working with civilians. (This in fact was the limited role which was all that was foreseen in the time of Knox's adjutant-generalcy (1935–37), when it was suggested that all the woman-power necessary could be obtained through the Ministry of Labour without the added complication of forming a women's service.) There can be no doubt, however, that what the women liked, however humdrum the duties were, was a closer identification than this with the unit they supported. This, and the belief that they were trusted to do a good job, was one of the pillars on which their morale rested.

A strong link was forged between the ATS and the air defence regiments of the Royal Artillery through the foresight of General Pile who, ahead of his time, believed that women were capable of many skilled tasks around the battery position, which in due course led to the establishment of mixed batteries. This coopera-tion started pre-war in Territorial training, where there was none of the feelings of strangeness and resentment aroused by the intrusion of women into a strictly masculine world, because the Territorials were already quite accustomed to working with the opposite sex in their ordinary civilian employment, and both sexes were already acclimatized. The long and happy association between the ATS and the Gunners is told in a later chapter.

Things were generally better for all specialists, such as the other ATS employed with the artillery in proof and experimental establishments – women proved adept at using kine-theodolites, for instance – linguists and officers trained for special intelligence duties.

One of the earliest and biggest ATS operations – perhaps more properly one should say ATS–FANY operations – was the staffing of a large part of the vehicle side of the Central Ordnance Depot at Chilwell, to which all kinds of vehicles and spare parts were collected from industry and from which they were delivered all over the country and to ports of embarkation to bring units up to their mobilization scales. The companies deployed there were originally all mixed companies without drivers, while the FANY driver companies were apt not to have any cooks or clerks for their own support, so a rapid change of employment had to be arranged for those women who were found to be able to drive a car, and civilian volunteers who could drive were rapidly enrolled without ceremony and kitted up as best they could be, as apart from procrastination over authorized scales there was a great shortage of everything, especially of greatcoats in the first very cold winter of 1939–40.

Chilwell was one of the early ATS Groups, a Group ATS being a formation of a varying number of companies brigaded together as was convenient, so that their administration could be supervised by a Senior Commandant ATS (major), who at Chilwell was A. R. Gell. She carried a huge work load, billeting, paying and looking after the domestic economy of her floating population: sometimes her drivers were away for days at a time on their long trips to factory or docks.

The women took over a complicated industrial process, receiving indents, preparing the vehicles demanded for the road – which meant, if consigned overseas, stripping them down and putting all 'attractive' stores in packing cases and nailing them down (there was a black market in things like seats, mirrors, windscreen wipers, batteries, tyres and tools – and theft on a considerable scale), preparing vouchers and vehicle documents and finally delivering them to the drivers in running order.

The drivers themselves lived a strenuous life, working a seven-day week, but they and the FANY in particular, were by education and temperament inclined to working without supervision and on their own. Others found the FANY sense of their own superiority irritating, but as is the case in all armies this is one of the foundations of *esprit de corps*.

A typical day (following one account) might start in billets with the landlady banging on the door on a bitter winter's morning at 6 a.m. and throwing clothes and boots, soaked in the previous day's run and airing in the kitchen all night, in the girls' bedroom with a cry of 'They're done to a turn'. A hasty breakfast and then dressing in the improvised survival kit of the day— two pairs of stockings, two pairs of socks, pyjama trousers, battledress trousers, and the shirt and battledress blouse augmented by a sweater, a scarf, an issue greatcoat, if lucky, and a sheepskin jacket overall, with a balaclava helmet and hat to keep the head warm, and the obligatory steel helmet hitched on to the obligatory respirator, anti-gas to make all complete. Then out into the snow and into the vast vehicle reception station full of blazing lights, chattering girls, revving engines and section leaders trying to call the roll above the din, to collect vehicle and documents and six shillings billeting money for each night out.

As convoy drivers the motor companies were seen to be remarkably efficient. The combat army spent a great deal of its time practising convoy drill, it being found that soldiers until trained could lose themselves or break down on any journey over five miles, and they required to be navigated by officers, shepherded by motor-cyclists who planted signs all over the place while the lame ducks were collected by the REME break-down trucks nursing the rear. From time to time such exercises were enlivened by meeting one of those long convoys of stripped down, new 15 cwt or 3 ton trucks, often without cab or tilt—hence the bundle of clothes—sailing happily along at well-kept intervals and driven by squads of attractive girls, perfectly self-sufficient and unmoved by chaff or whistles. But as the war went on the women were taken for granted as being a natural part of the army.

Once the British Expeditionary Force had had time to settle down in France it was planned to deploy two groups of ATS

8   Integration

9   *The first party of ATS to arrive in Normandy, July, 1944*

10   HRH The Princess Royal visits women of Anti-Aircraft Command (TA) Weyborne, 1951

11   HM The Queen, when Princess Elizabeth: she was commissioned into the ATS in March, 1945

on the lines of communication. The Director, Dame Helen, went out in December to make the necessary arrangements, receiving a far more cordial welcome than she had twenty-two years earlier. She and the two senior administrative officers were well known to each other. Whitehead, her old friend and staunch ally of former days, was now a brigadier in the Deputy Adjutant-General's department, and General Lord Gort's own daughter was a member of her staff in the War Office. (It is difficult to trace the identity of all the senior officers of that period, but it is clear from the coincidence of many surnames that the ridiculous idea of the earlier war that the 'truly feminine woman' did not join the women's services had been reversed. It must have been a great advantage to have, as many military wives did, some practical experience in women's welfare, and also to have a shared social outlook and idiom with army officers. Senior Commandant Wagstaff, for instance, was the wife of a former commandant of the Royal Military Academy, Woolwich.)

The first ATS detachment to arrive in France was a platoon of bilingual telephonists, for Paris. It was followed by two groups, one under Senior Commandant J. K. S. Ince, FANY, based on Dieppe, and the other under Senior Commandant Wagstaff, at Nantes. HQ Lines of Communication was at Le Mans, and it will be noted that in contrast to 1917–18 the base and lines of communication area stretched far to the west and was not concentrated by the Pas de Calais. This was fortunate, because when the Allied defence system north of the Somme collapsed under the blitzkrieg it enabled the large force of valuable troops to the south and all the lines of communication to be safely evacuated.

There is really little to be said about the short stay of the ATS in France in 1940 except to record that as might be expected they did their duty without flap or fuss, the contribution of the FANY ambulance drivers being especially noted. Dieppe was severely bombed but fortunately only one battle casualty is recorded in the whole period—wounded and evacuated. It soon became clear that any hope of establishing a new front in France

5

was illusory, and all the women were first withdrawn from Dieppe and then, as the extent of the French moral collapse became clear, evacuated at short notice. The ATS had their share of misadventures, either forcing their vehicles through roads crowded with refugees or being jolted in trains, with uncertain schedules and destinations. One party was hitched to an east-bound train but spotted the mistake before it was delivered to what remained of a front. Commandant Ince collected twenty-two FANY ambulance drivers who arrived after five days on the road and put them to work in Nantes, from whence they were evacuated, with Commandant Wagstaff's group, via Rennes and St Malo, which involved a difficult journey across the refugee routes. So short was the notice to pack up and go that the main body had to leave Nantes before the girls who were having their afternoon off could be collected, and they were rounded up later by Commandant Wagstaff, who brought the last straggler on by car. The telephone platoon attached to the Royal Signals in Paris had to walk the last stage as the mobs on the road made all vehicle movement impossible. After these minor misadventures every ATS was embarked on the crowded SS *Royal Sovereign* — there were two hospitals on board and emergency surgery was continued in a make-shift theatre 'tween decks — and they arrived safely in England on 16 June.

In July Commandant Chitty was sent out to the Middle East to see if it was practical to enrol the women, all British Army wives or dependents, working in GHQ or in HQ British Troops in Egypt, into the ATS. Why this was thought desirable is not clear, for if it was to bring civilians who had access to a mass of sensitive information under firmer military control this would not have been achieved by putting them into uniform as the ATS disciplinary code at that time was toothless. In any case the situation was so threatening that it seemed a better policy to repatriate the families, not retain them. Apart from which, the atmosphere in Cairo at that time was such that the ladies in question had no intention of surrendering their independence or their civilian status. Commandant Chitty remained to help out an overworked and harassed staff with family repatriation, herself returning via South Africa in the *Empress of Britain*, spending seven hours in an open boat in the Altantic when that fine ship was torpedoed. She returned to take the post of Assistant Director in GHQ Middle East Forces in 1941 when the ATS build-up had reached respectable proportions.

The first detachment to be sent out from England were twenty ATS officers trained in technical intelligence duties for the Combined Services Detailed Interrogation Centre at Maadi, outside Cairo, in December, 1940, together with a small contingent of cooks and mess orderlies under Company Commander K. Morrison Bell, as the need for security ruled out the employment of any locally recruited staff.

So by the end of 1940 the women's service was firmly at grips with its many tasks. Whatever it was doing, it was doing well, and the rest of the army saw it was doing its job well. The result was a call from almost every branch for ATS transport. At the end of the year Anti-Aircraft Command, where the women's service had fully justified General Pile's belief in their potential, was some 19,000 men short of establishment and he wanted 8,500 more women at once. But at the outbreak of the war the whole ATS was only some 17,000 strong (914 officers and 16,000 rank and file in August, to be precise) and in December it was only double this (it was to reach 207,492 three years later), and for one reason or another recruiting, still voluntary, was drying up, the rate of discharge was high, and there were signs of sagging morale now that the first excitements of the war were over and boredom, the blackout and the blitz began to make their effects felt. There had undeniably been mistakes, and there was a good deal of discontent, not only in the women's service but in the new hastily raised army of citizens as a whole. Looking back, the way the ATS had coped and the way the senior officers had made such a ramshackle structure work at all without any real disciplinary sanctions is beyond praise, but at the time there was a great deal of public anxiety, and publicity, much of it hostile. This state of affairs was directly due to the long delay in setting up the service and the panic haste with which it was finally done, but then there is seldom much justice in war. The mistakes had made themselves felt and the time was now ripe for a drastic overhaul of the leadership and organization of the whole Service.

Chapter V

Two Hundred Thousand Women

THE year 1940 had begun with blank ignorance of the nature of modern war, followed by the disasters in France, the return of the Army defeated and virtually disarmed, the opening of the 'blitz' — 1075 civilians were killed in August alone — the Battle of Britain and the threat of invasion. All the same there was, as those who lived through those days will recall, a curious mood of optimism, even of triumph over adverse circumstances, born of relief, that things could not turn out much worse. We may have been ejected ignominiously from the continent of Europe, but the armed forces had not disgraced themselves and were safely back at home. The dark fears of a repetition of the blood-baths of 1916–18 had not been fulfilled. We had been bombed and blitzed, and yet in spite of pre-war predictions the country was still standing up. For a great many young, raw soldiers the war was still exciting and novel — a sort of prolonged Territorial training camp in a glorious summer with a distant threat of real action to lend point to much hard training and hard physical work preparing defences. For all the muddle and confusion, this mood was shared by their sisters in the ATS, whether they were extracting themselves from France in their unflappable way, driving their vehicles or acclimatizing themselves to life with the anti-aircraft batteries deployed in the field.

In 1941 the mood had changed. Propaganda and morale-building apart, the time had come to look closely at all the defects in the war machine and say good-bye to muddle and dauntless amateurism. This was not to be done in a few months; in fact it was to take two long years, but it was in 1941 that the foundations of the victories of 1943 and 1944 were laid. It was also the year in which the Women's Service was finally transformed from what was no more than a body of uniformed camp-followers* to a true Service, a partner in the armed forces and a full member of the Army.

On 10 April, 1941, the Secretary of State for War announced in Parliament that 'The Auxiliary Territorial Service has proved so valuable to the Army in replacement of men that the Government have decided to increase its numbers greatly and to enlarge the range of duties it performed. Members of the Service are already discharging important functions connected with the Air Defence of Great Britian as well as with the rest of the forces at home, and these are of a character that renders it desirable that the volunteers performing them should be definitely declared members of the Armed Forces of the Crown. The whole Service will accordingly be given full military status. Women will, of course, be employed only on work for which they have special aptitude, but the House should know that such work includes duties at searchlight gun stations . . . The Service will remain a women's service, under the general direction of women, and the disciplinary code will only be applied to it in so far as the wider responsibilities now envisaged necessitate.' In effect this meant that the strength of the Service was to be raised to 200,000 all ranks.

Here was a laconic but tremendous tribute to the Service, and a vindication of the long, uphill struggle to create it, in whose van Dame Helen had fought so well and so selflessly for so long. Ironically it coincided with the decision by the same Secretary of State to relieve her as Director ATS in the War Office. To put this event in its correct perspective it must be remembered that when winter followed the exciting summer and autumn of 1940 the whole army began to feel the impact of continued separation from wives and families, the black-out, life in uncomfortable camps and billets and the dull slog of military routine. It is when danger is past and real action is only a distant prospect that the

---

* The term 'camp-followers' has a derogatory ring, but it has a precise meaning, and that is what the WAAC, the QMAAC and at first the ATS in fact were.

soldier, male or female, has time to discover how uncomfortable he or she is and how irritating the minor constraints of military life. There was a lot of discontent—about 'bull', about welfare, mal-administration of the disciplinary code, poor leadership, poor management, and the selection of officers, and there is no doubt that a lot of it was justified; there were bound to be mistakes made when creating a huge citizen army. Leadership and management are part of the professional equipment of an officer, and have to be learnt like any other skills, and it took time. The citizen army being raised for the Second World War was not, like the New Armies of the Great War, isolated in camps buried in the country or in a theatre of war overseas. It spilled over into the towns and cities. Units lived in close contact and mixed intimately with civilians. As a result the Army came under the close scrutiny of a jealous public—a public sympathetic to the Royal Navy and the Royal Air Force but traditionally hostile to the 'military'—and every fault and minor injustice was immediately visible and immediately noticed. There was a sustained campaign against the army, often exaggerated, often misinformed, but, it must be added, although it was resented at the time by many officers, it had the valuable effect of exposing some obsolete attitudes and practices, and it brought home the need for good public relations, an idea then novel, even repugnant, to many army officers.

This was only a passing phase. The morale of the army remained high throughout the war, even when things were at their lowest ebb. In its regular core it possessed a reservoir of experience in man-management and leadership on which the wartime officers could draw, and at the top the chair of the Adjutant-General, who is especially concerned with such matters, was occupied by one of the ablest and most humane men ever to occupy it, General Sir Ronald Adam. The ATS was far from being in so favourable a position. As we have seen, it had been brought into being too late and too hurriedly. There were many able women in it who were potentially good officers, but none had any more training than had been provided by 'Emergency Service' and the short five day courses run before the war started at the Duke of York's Headquarters. (The Cadet Wing was not formed until December, 1939, and the first Officer Cadet Training Unit, ATS, until February 1941.) Many officers had been appointed and promoted for the sole reason that they were available and willing to serve and for their social standing. There were no confidential reports or gradings, and like the male Territorial Army, senior officers were often reluctant to apply the ruthless standards of the regular army to friends whom they knew socially in civil life.

Almost all the military knowledge and 'know-how' was concentrated in the Director, who had no trained staff officers and only a small and rudimentary machine through which to exercise command and control. Her trusted Deputy Controller, Christian Fraser-Tytler, and the greater part of her Directorate had been moved to Cheltenham in conformity with the policy to disperse War Office branches to the provinces to avoid bombing. This led to a form of dual control, as frequently the Deputy had to take decisions for lack of time to refer the question to her Director in London, which made for difficulties, even with the best will in the world, when there were so many matters of essential detail to attend to.

The difficulty about 'A', the Adjutant-General's side of staff-work, is that while 'G', or operations, can be decided according to general military principles and 'Q' by good managerial skills and calculations, in 'A', which deals with human beings, every problem is an individual one. Leslie Whateley, who was to be Director in her turn, has described how she was hurled suddenly from the task of a company assistant (second-lieutenant) to the equivalent of a DAAG in the War Office with, among her tasks, the allocation of recruits by trades from the initial training centres to Army units: 'A jigsaw puzzle made more complicated by the pieces of the puzzle changing their shapes overnight'. She also describes how every complaint was aimed at the ATS Directorate, from whom the worried parent expected an immediate reply, whereas by standard practice it was circulated first to whichever of the War Office Directorates appeared to be primarily concerned. (This she was later instrumental in altering, so that a sensible and sympathetic reply promising attention and written in English rather than the evasive jargon of the Civil Service was sent at once.)

The point was that while it could be reasonably argued that the men were being trained for the rigours of active service and that they should, up to a point, be prepared to grin and bear it, this was quite impossible to advance to mothers of every class worrying about their daughters. The first wave of women volunteers were, like their Territorial Army comrades as a whole, intelligent, adventurous, adaptable and full of the initiative. The second were only volunteers in a technical sense, having been 'directed' to the ATS by the Ministry of Labour and National Service, and excellent material as they were, they came from less privileged classes, had never been away from home or shared a communal life, didn't know how to look after themselves and were even frightened of the dark. To reassure them, train them and then look after them in their units was too often the responsibility of officers who were badly in need of training and guidance themselves. In all fairness to the ATS officers who came under such criticism it must be added that there was a national muddle in which there were miscalculations in the equation connecting requirements of recruits, facilities for training them and operational vacancies into which trained women could be fitted. Accommodation was short, and yet somehow unposted auxiliaries had to be retained in holding platoons, which are always a potential source of indiscipline because of boredom and lack of work. This situation was aggravated by the proportion of unmotivated dullards and hard cases in the 'directed' recruits.

The Directorate lacked any Public Relations Staff, vital in such a context, bearing in mind that it was not only the morale of the Service that was at stake but of the public as a whole. The result was that for a long period, well into 1942, the Service was continually under fire from Parliament, Press and the people. Dame Helen's own position was weakened by the Report of the Defence Sub-Committee of the Parliamentary Select Committee on Expenditure who looked into the administration of the Services and reported adversely on the ATS officers and especially on the lack of imagination and energy they had shown over obtaining good accommodation, meals, rest, recreation and welfare generally.

In November, 1939, the Duchess of Northumberland had inaugurated an ATS comforts fund which provided many amenities. The Chaplain-General had sponsored a women's committee for religious work at ATS training centres; some small funds were made available for the women's companies for games and sports equipment, for the new units had had no chance to build up their private 'PRI funds'. Religious organizations like the YWCA, the Church Army and the Salvation Army were available to help but, as the Markham Report was to point out, it is not enough for regimental officers to wait for manna from the charitable organizations to fall on them; welfare requires to be fought for using imagination, resource and even aggression.

Dame Helen herself, deeply respected and admired as she was for her great ability and selfless devotion to duty, was feared and disliked in many quarters. Fundamentally sensitive and feminine – one has only to look at the portrait by Philip de Laszlo of the beautiful young Helen Fraser, or the photographs of the frail and distinguished old lady she became – she had a forthright manner and a rough tongue. She suffered no one gladly, let alone fools. (Leslie Whateley recalls what a ticking off she received from her when still green in the War Office, for the heinous crime of using the *first* instead of the *third* person in an inter-branch minute!) Khaki uniform is not one of the most becoming of outfits, especially on a lady of 62, but Dame Helen, with the intellectual's contempt for appearance, seemed in her voluminous ill-fitting skirt and jacket, her gaiters, her cap with its long peak pulled down over her fine eyes, her jaw jutting as she stumped down a line of auxiliaries paraded for inspection, as if she was modelling herself on the cruel cartoons of women officers by Osbert Lancaster or 'Pont'. Her God was efficiency, and her soul's aim was still the advancement of women by proving what they could do. It would be unfair to say that she was indifferent to welfare, but she was a Victorian, brought up in a school where discomfort was believed to strengthen the character and to be ill – she was never ill herself – was indicative of lack of moral fibre. Great as her gifts were she was against any compromise on what she believed to be sound principles, and she was not easy to work with. She had not taken kindly to the broadly based advisory council set up to assist the Directorate and the War Office in ATS matters.

All high military appointments are political to some degree and the head of the Women's Service was politically an extremely sensitive one. The Secretary of State, Captain Margesson, himself an ex-soldier with a manner as blunt as Dame Helen's own, sent for her in March and informed her that he intended to replace her, a decision she accepted with her customary dignity and stoicism. Her last and signal service was to suggest to Captain Margesson the name of Mrs Jean Knox (later Lady Swaythling) as a possible successor. The arrangement made was that Senior Commandant (Major) Knox was to be promoted Controller (Colonel) and appointed temporarily Inspector ATS, enabling her to visit units in the field with the necessary authority to examine what she pleased, ask what questions she liked, and form her own opinion of the many problems to be tackled. This appointment would lapse and after a short period she would then be promoted Chief-Controller (major-general) and appointed Director, ATS. This was effected on 21 July, 1941. So passed from the scene a relentless fighter for the cause of women, the original architect of the Corps we have today, and one of the most distinguished women of her era.

The new Director represented not only a break with tradition but a complete change in style. All that she had in common with her predecessor was a clear brain and tremendous energy and drive. Her public image was exactly right for a young service; she was just over 30 years old, very attractive, smartly and immaculately turned out and highly articulate. No one was better fitted to lend panache to the ATS role, uniform and cap badge. This was a much needed improvement in the image and excellent for public relations. As well, she possessed the right kind of experience, having worked first as a company commander and then in the

War Office in AG 18 under the Director of Recruiting, and so had gained the essential understanding of how the machine worked. She had a quick mind, an unerring sense of priorities and the supreme gift of being able to delegate.

The appointment of her Deputy was equally fortunate. Senior Commander Leslie Whateley (later Dame Leslie, to become Director in 1943) was second in seniority to Commandant Fraser-Tytler, the Deputy Director who was based with the main part of the Directorate which had been moved out of London to Chelten-ham. She had already carried a lot of responsibility and her work had led to frequent contact with the retiring Director. She too was a gifted woman, equally determined as her dynamic new chief, but quieter in style and with the insight into ATS affairs and public reaction conferred through being herself the wife of a serving officer in the RAF and the mother of a son about to enter the army. In the restructured Directorate the Cheltenham wing would continue as before, but the new Deputy would hold the fort in London, in close touch with all the branches concerned, keeping fully in her Director's mind and taking decisions on her behalf. The Director herself concentrated on visiting the units in the field, yet meeting frequently to exchange views and discuss policy. They were to prove a well-matched team. The first task they decided to tackle was to remove any grounds on which the cam-paign of rumour — the 'whispering campaign' as Dame Leslie has called it — and the adverse press publicity was based, and to counter-attack with positive propaganda based on the facts and the real achievements of the Service. At the same time there was a heavy load of straight staff duties required to bring about the momentous change announced by the Secretary of State for War in April.

Basically what had to be done was this. First the whole Service had to be brought into the Army which meant that they were to become subject to the Army Act. This was brought about by Army Council Instruction of 19 June, 1941, under Regulation 6 of the Defence (Women's Forces) Regulations, 1941. Second, by an Order in Council (30 May, 1941) women were henceforth to be commissioned as officers in the same way as male officers of the Army. Third as a Service, the ATS staff structure and arrangements for command and control, bearing in mind its unique nature as a female organization, had to be broght in line with the well-tried methods used for the other Corps and Service in the War Office and with field force units and static establishments. Fourth, the whole process of measuring aptitudes, selection and allocation of skills and aptitudes to jobs of the intakes of recruits had to be modernized, so as to ensure that the officers were in fact potentially good leaders, and that there was an economical and rational use of women-power. Fifth, the machinery for all this had to be set up to do all this *and* at the same time to train the new intake, which meant turning out the skilled personnel to man the necessary training establishments of which sixteen were brought into being in 1941 alone and no fewer than forty-two at some time or another during the war.

To give some idea of the magnitude of the task, imagine that the whole British army in 1941 had consisted of only one division with just sufficient ancillary troops to back it, and it was then ordered to expand tenfold, which would be equivalent to a force substantially bigger than the whole British Army today, in a year. This, in fact, was what was done.

As regards the first step the authorities had to take into account the nature of the Service and public sensitivity to the question of subjecting women to what, in the popular imagination, was the harsh military code of discipline. Briefly, and in imprecise, non-legal terms what the Army Council did (by virtue of regulation 6 of the Defence (Women's Forces) Regulations of 1941) was to bring the ATS under just so many penal sections of the Army Act and rules of procedure as would serve to maintain discipline, together with such special provisos and restrictions as would allay any public fears of harshness or hazarding women to the full rigour of the Act. At that time all the women were volunteers and desertion was not a crime. (The rules were changed and strengthened in some detail when the Order in Council of March the following year brought in the conscription of women.) Section

15 enabled an absentee to be apprehended and returned to her unit under escort, and the only other applicable section was that famous catch-all Section 40 relating to 'conduct to the prejudice of good order and military discipline',* the adjective 'military' being dropped for women, for some reason not now apparent. Punishments were mild, being limited to admonition, reprimand, confinement to barracks up to 14 days, forfeiture of pay up to 14 days, and stoppages of up to £4 to make good damage to government equipment by loss or neglect (Section 138). In accordance with the Army Act any summary award involving a financial penalty could at the accused's request be referred to trial by court-martial. The privates (or 'auxiliaries', as they were officially termed) had an additional safeguard in that they could not be remanded for trial by court-martial, but could only be so tried if the accused herself so elected. (This was opposed to the Act as it applied to males, for whom some offences could only be tried by court-martial, or who could be remanded for court-martial thereby becoming liable for a higher penalty than could be imposed summarily. Officers, warrant officers and NCOs were liable to trial by court-martial, with the maximum penalties of dismissal from the Service for the officers and discharge for the rest. Disciplinary powers over women could only be exercised by ATS officers, or by male general officers holding the specific appointments of area or divisional commanders, which meant in effect of the rank of major-general or above.)

This was a very mild code, reflecting the feeling inside the service that the women's service was composed of highly motivated volunteers whose discipline was self-discipline and based on morale and good leadership, and the feeling of the public outside the service that the application of anything resembling the military penal code with all its unpleasant associations in the public mind to women was unsuitable and highly repugnant. Both were understandable but mistaken. Once the ATS began to expand and women were directed into it, it was open, like the rest of the army,

* The current version of the Act is different and the old familiar numbers no longer apply.

to entry by the whole spectrum of behaviour, and the motivation inspired by good leadership and training had to have the backing of a disciplinary code. The solid evidence of history is that the ATS were extraordinarily well behaved, and this fact will be emphasized throughout the book, but it would be foolish to pretend that the auxiliaries were all angels, and mealy-mouthed to conceal that an appreciable number of hard cases passed through its ranks, capable of regularly breaking out of confinement, assaulting their superior officers and guilty of theft and prostitution. There was always trouble over absenteeism. Sanctions were essential to preserve 'good order and military discipline', even if this was only detection and discharge. Every military body, however democratic the society from which it is drawn – and which it is designed to protect, requires a disciplinary code in which both rights and duties are spelt out, which is understood by all ranks, and seen to be fair and fairly applied. Bringing the Service under the Army Act was therefore an important measure in transforming it into a truly military body as opposed to a society of amateurs.

On 5 March, 1942, the final identification of the women's with the men's service was taken when by Order in Council under the provisions of the *National Service Acts, 1939 to 1941,* women, except for certain safeguarded categories, became liable to be called up for service with the armed forces like their husbands and brothers. The extremely important subject of pay was also brought into line with the Army's code in April, 1941. Women were only allowed two-thirds of the men's basic emoluments, but 'staff' pay for the appointment of adjutant was admissible, so was 'corps' pay for those with the necessary qualifications for women working with Royal Enginners, the Royal Signals, the Royal Army Service Corps and the Royal Electrical and Mechanical Engineers. Auxiliaries became eligible for tradesmen's rates of pay and proficiency pay on the same conditions as all other soldiers.

These changes were symbolized by the rationalization of uniform, badges of rank, arm of the service, affiliation and trade. These were brought into line with the rest of the Army, and the dual nature of the Service indicated by the wearing of the ATS cap-badge, the ATS or FANY flash as a shoulder title, the ATS lanyard of chocolate brown, beech brown and green, and the badge of the regiment or corps supported above the left breast pocket. The ATS serving with the Royal Artillery also wore the white lanyard of the Gunners. (Inappropriately but honourably, as they were never allowed to serve in the detachment (crew) of a gun. The RA lanyard is the stylized version of the cord once used to hook on the lock of a gun to fire it.) The uniform eventually ran to a vocabulary of eighteen printed pages running from 'Anklets ATS' to 'Vests, string (for snow areas)'. One footnote gave exact instructions on how the ten garments from long pants to windproof smock for extreme cold conditions were to be donned, and the next section begins with the authority for issue of slouch hats and sandals for auxiliaries bound for India and the Far East.

The WOs and NCOs were called by their normal army titles but recognition stopped short of giving the officers army ranks as the Women's Royal Army Corps uses now, and a modified version of the titles in use was adopted:

Army	*ATS*
Major-General	Chief Controller
Brigadier	Senior Controller
Colonel	Controller
Lieutenant-Colonel	Chief Commander
Major	Senior Commander
Captain	Junior Commander
Lieutenant	Subaltern
Second Lieutenant	Second Subaltern

(The officers' badges of rank were the same as the men's.)

All the officers were commissioned formally:

'GEORGE,
By the Grace of God of Great Britian, Ireland and the British Dominions beyond the seas King, Defender of the Faith,

12   WRAC Band, Brandenburg Gate, Berlin

13   HRH the Princess Royal with the Director and ex-Directors of the Corps, Golden Jubilee, 1967. Back Row, left to right, Brigadier J. E. Henderson, Brigadier Dame Jean Rivett–Drake, Brigadier Dame Mary Railton, Brigadier Dame Mary Colvin, Brigadier Dame Francis Coulshed, Brigadier Dame Mary Tyrwhitt. Front Row, left to right, Dame Helen Gwynne Vaughan, The Princess Royal, Brigadier Dame Leslie Whateley

14   Brigadier Eileen Nolan inspecting a guard of honour, Woolwich, 1975

*15   Colonel L. M. Davies CBE in the winner's enclosure after Midsummer
Lad had won the Thrush Handicap Stakes at Kempton, 1975*

Emperor of India . . . To our trusty and well beloved . . . Greeting! We, reposing especial trust and confidence in your loyalty, courage and good conduct, do by these presents constitute and appoint you to be an officer in our Auxiliary Territorial Service . . . in the rank of second subaltern or in such other rank as We may from time to time hereafter be pleased to promote or appoint you to . . . '

and then appointed war substantive, temporary or acting in the rank at which they had reached on the date of formal commission.

Sorting out the officers was a great problem requiring tact, humanity and firmness. A proper system of reporting had to be introduced and the whole corps winnowed over, retrained in their basic skills if necessary, reported on and, if they did not make the grade, disposed of. It was found necessary that officers commissioned purely on the basis of a skill in the early days of emergency had, if they were to be effective, good 'regimental' officers as well, and they too had to be retrained. A Junior Officers School was opened in April and a Senior Officers School in October, 1942. Here a difficulty arose which illustrates the basic difference in the attitude of women – at least then, in that highly formative period – and men, and the need for a female command chain. Men, except the unusually sensitive or ambitious, set no great store by course reports, and accepted a 'stinker' with resignation or even, one regrets to say, with amusement. Their sisters, more sensitive and more conscientious, were deeply depressed by a critical report, to say nothing of an 'adverse' or a low grading. Acute nervousness afflicted perfectly capable junior commanders and subalterns ordered to attend, and they had to be patiently taught that course reports, like confidential reports, were not fatal and final verdicts, but afforded an insight to the officer on her own abilities and a guide to her future employment.

Cadets for officer training had so far been selected in the traditional manner by recommendation by commanding officers and interview by a selection board of senior ATS officers. The Army had found this to be inadequate. Commanding officers all had quite

6

different standards, many had a strong bias in favour of one social type and others tended to withhold recommendation for fear of losing good men—or women. A widespread screening was inaugurated to discover the badly needed officer potential hidden in the ranks. In this the ATS followed suit, and a slightly modified version of the new methods of selection for male officers was adopted.

The short, fifteen-minute interview by an untrained board was subjective, influenced too much by the board's personal prejudices and discovered little about the true potential or character weaknesses of the candidate. Failure rates at the OCTU became alarmingly high. The new methods, brought into effect from 1943 onwards, were an examination in depth designed with psychological advice with the special tasks of an ATS officer in view and consisted of the interview, observation of the group of candidates over two or three days in social and mess life, educational and intelligence tests and 'leaderless' group tests.

Selection of the rank and file was a question of testing for basic intelligence and then for special aptitudes, and a battery of suitable tests was devised similar to those used for men known as 'S.P.' tests. Non-commissioned officers and warrant officers were produced in the traditional way by local promotion and learning on the job, but as well a WO's and NCO's School was opened in May, 1941, which proved invaluable and remained open until the end of the war.

Basic training at the ATS Training Centres, of which there were twenty-two altogether at one time or another (four and a half weeks), WO and NCO training (four weeks), officer cadet training at the OCTUs (eight weeks), junior officers (four weeks) and senior officers (four weeks) which provided the foundation of the whole Service were the responsibility of the Director, ATS. As well the ATS Directorate scripted an outstanding training film for the benefit of officers illustrating the correct principles of command and leadership. It was called *We Serve* and starred, among others, Joyce Redman, Norah Swinburne, Googie Withers, Celia Johnson and Ann Todd, and was directed by Carol Reed. A private showing to an audience of senior officials and people in the public service demonstrated how well the ATS understood its business and it was admired and borrowed by the Director of the WAAF.

While all this was being put in hand the machinery for command and control was being reorganized. It should be borne in mind that the heads, or directors, of each 'service', i.e. those branches of the army which 'serve' the principal combat arms in the field, have as a chief the appropriate member of the Army Council, and the Director ATS dealing with people, as opposed to *things*, came under the Adjutant-General. The Director does not command his service, but is responsible to his chief for its specialist skills. Inside the War Office trained staff officers from the service are included in other branches — notably Training (MT) — where professional advice is required. The units of the service or 'corps' are fitted into the normal command structure of the Army, with 'deputy directors' advising at a high level — e.g. at Army or Command or theatre. Lower down the hierarchy the commanders of units double the role of specialist adviser to their formation or equivalent commander. Discipline is a general army matter: the appropriate skills a matter of the heads of service.

The position of the ATS was similar, but the responsibilities exactly the opposite. Technical proficiency was the responsibility of the Directorate of Military Training and the appropriate 'arm' e.g., the Royal Artillery, or 'service' — the Royal Electrical and Mechanical Engineers, all down the line. The Director ATS and her officers were responsible for the morale, welfare, 'well-being' — a favourite ATS term — 'tone', and not least important, their public image. In this last the ATS differed from the nursing service, their ancillaries the British Red Cross Society and the VADs, and a small number of ATS who were trained as nursing orderlies and clinical clerks. The nurses' role was the traditional and accepted feminine one of caring for the sick and wounded; their battles for recognition had been fought and won in the historical past, and they were high in the public esteem. It was the 'army' of women, dressed and behaving like soldiers that caught public attention and anxiety, in spite of the fact that they could claim with pride that as far as they were soldiers there were no others in the Army quieter, better behaved and better disciplined.

Briefly, the DATS set-up after reorganization was as follows. The Director was, as said, responsible to the Adjutant-General and was served by three sections, AG 15 (Military Secretary matters, relating to individual officers), AG 19 (welfare and well-being) and AG 20 (ATS training, i.e. basic, as opposed to specialist, technical skills.) She was supported by a Senior Controller as Deputy and anchor woman in the Directorate (Leslie Whateley) but later there were two: Senior Controller M. Baxter Ellis (AG 15 and 20) and Senior Controller Jackson (AG 19). The ATS was represented in two other Adjutant-General's Directorates: the Directorate of Organization by AG 16 and the Directorate of Selection of Personnel by S.P. 1, 2 and 3.

Medical advice was all-important, not only for advice on health, exercise and hygiene, but medical opinion was a useful lever for obtaining agreement to improvements in ATS living conditions. Lieutenant-Colonel Albertine Winner of the RAMC attended all the main ATS conferences and supported the Service 'as wholeheartedly as if she had been a member of it'.

These may seem all dry facts, but it must be remembered that while a regiment or corps may be remembered by its deeds, these deeds are only made possible by a sound staff structure and much careful preparation and hard work. There is one other point to be made. The Service was run from the top by women. A very senior Civil Servant, enquiring demi-officially into the way the ATS Directorate worked, asked Senior Controller Whateley which senior Civil Servant was advising them on how to conduct their affairs (a normal and useful part of the set-up of a Service ministry) and finding there was none, remarked that she must have an unusually gifted staff. That was indeed borne out by the results.

We must now return to the subject of the 'whispering campaign'. Jean Knox and Leslie Whateley spent long hours discussing every possible measure to make the Service proof against accusation or rumour of bad personnel management. The battle was won, as such battles always are, not by any single striking measure but by steady improvements made on a wide front, but some key measures must be mentioned. First, there is no substitute in administration of any kind for constant, searching inspection by an inspecting officer who knows what she is looking for. The arrangement by which the Director roved in the field and the Deputy stood in for her with frequent meetings for discussion and regular conferences of senior officers from the Commands was responsible for much of the success. The training of officers, especially senior officers, was equally important.

A valuable contribution was made by the Markham Committee, composed of distinguished ladies and gentlemen under the chairmanship of the self-same woman who had been secretary of the committee of enquiry into the morals of the WAAC in 1917, Miss Violet Markham, CH. It was set up as a result of the public anxiety caused by the Press and the 'whispering campaign' in February, 1942, to look into the welfare of all three women's services and to make recommendations. It produced, in August, an extremely candid report containing severe criticisms and much sound advice, but owing to the powerful intellect of the chairman and her relentless search for facts and insistence on tracing every rumour to its source, and if necessary exploding it, the whole atmosphere was thoroughly cleared. Violet Markham has been described as a women of seventy with the energy of one of forty, the extra years serving only to enrich her experience of life, and who combined her great ability with complete lack of conceit and profound understanding of human nature, whose services to the women's service and the ATS were immense.

In the public relations, however, mere reputation is not enough. Much of what was going round was both malicious and extremely unpleasant, and it is a sad fact that people relish unpleasant rumours, especially in wartime; also that they are too often actually reinforced by investigative journalism, whose motives may be entirely praiseworthy, but whose demands for the facts and repetition of the rumour only serve to spread it more widely. This sometimes leads disinterested parties to imagine that if the rumours were entirely groundless the Press would hardly bother with them.

Quite apart from complaints about lack of welfare, bad personnel management and bad living conditions, many of which were justified but were being corrected, there were other damaging and malicious stories in circulation. There were revivals of the accusations of immorality and mass discharges due to illegitimate pregnancy. Both were false and required to be refuted. It was sadly true that the war revealed that in twentieth-century prosperous Britain, part of the population were ignorant of some aspects of hygiene. (And for political reasons mention of this was avoided.) Scabies and head infestation were blamed on conditions in the ATS, when in fact the ATS having discovered the situation were working flat out to correct it, with education, medical measures, routine inspections and such practical steps as obtaining sanction for women's hairdressers on the establishment of units. (As a matter of social history, that much-maligned institution, the Army, introduced a large section of the population, male and female, to regular baths, oral hygiene, exercise, the maintenance of health and regular laundry.) Less unpleasant but annoying were such rumours as that girls were wandering about shopping and frequenting cafés when they should be working, when in fact they were night-shift workers; the list was endless. Thirty-five years after the event such stories may appear so trivial that sensible people should have ignored them, but they were too wide-spread and persistent to ignore, and women are by their nature far more vulnerable to this sort of sniping than men. They were a positive threat to morale and also a deterrent to recruiting. It was clear that a process of educating the public had to be put in hand.

The principles guiding public relations campaigns resemble those of war; the measures must be positive and aggressive and anticipate the 'enemy' moves. 'PR' is a professional skill. In February, 1942, a properly staffed section of the Directorate of Public Relations (PR 5) was set up to deal with ATS affairs. It took a grip of all interviews granted to the Press, provided a flow of news items ('stories') for the national and local newspapers – the latter being ever important – and managed the recruiting campaigns. ATS public relations officers were established in Commands. A Mobile

Exhibition Platoon and a Special Recruiting Platoon were organized and sent round the country, the smartness and intelligence of the girls making an excellent impression wherever they went. Their impact was greatly increased by the presence of the ATS band. A voluntary fife and drum band trained by the bandmaster of the Durham Light Infantry attended recruiting displays in Northern Command. This proved a success, so in May, 1942, a properly established corps of drums was approved, the first drum-major being Lorna Smith. Nine pipers, wearing the Hunting Stuart tartan by Royal permission, were later added to the buglers. Later reeds and strings were added, so the ATS possessed a corps of drums, buglers, pipers and music for a full military band capable of providing a small orchestra and a dance band.

Parties of ladies from organizations like the National Council of Women, the Women's Institute and the Women's Voluntary Service were taken round the ATS Training Centres to see conditions for themselves. A film starring Leslie Howard called *The Gentle Sex* with the Service as its theme was well received.

As regards the Press, one of the chief tormentors of the ATS was the Beaverbrook newspaper chain. That magnate, for all his drive and outstanding ability, was given to unaccountable, even irrational likes and dislikes, and these quirks were reflected in the policy of his editors. One of them was apparently ingrained hostility to the women's services. The Press as a whole was naturally taking a keen interest in the Markham Report and Mr Fearnley, an experienced press officer in PR5, seized the opportunity to arrange an interview between the Deputy Director, ATS and a representative of the *Sunday Express*, and this was successful to the extent that she was able to convince him that she welcomed complaints and the opportunity to deal with them, and that his paper should give publicity to this fact, and also that before publishing the details of a story it would be fair, and in the interests of good journalistic practice, if the Service was also allowed to have its say. Soon afterwards the rest of the Press fell in with this sensible arrangement. In this way the battle of public relations, and let there be no mistake it was a decisive battle which to have lost would have adversely affected the war effort, ended in victory.

The Royal family had remained far above the hurly-burly of political and PR infighting, but mention must be made of their unswerving support. The Princess Royal's private contribution in terms of wise counsel is a matter of history. Publicly, when all their other duties allowed, they made visits to establishments and attended parades. In July, 1942, for instance, the Princess Royal took the salute at a parade of the ATS in London District and attended their service in Westminster Abbey, and the Queen spent a day visiting ATS units in Southern Command.

The fifth anniversary of the Service in 1943 was greeted with acclaim at home and abroad. At home there was a representative parade in London and a service in Westminster Abbey at which the Commandant-in-Chief, H.M. the Queen, took the salute. In Bristol there was a parade at which Queen Mary took the salute, and the Princess Royal at another in York. There is no other occasion on which a Corps or Regiment of the British armed forces has been honoured to such a degree.

The successful outcome of the long struggle of 1942 and 1943 freed the leadership of the ATS to concentrate on their proper task of running the Service and enabling its units to devote themselves to the vast task of assisting in the preparations for the victories of 1944 and the return to North-West Europe. There was one notable casualty. The burden of work and anxiety for the two critical years had been carried by Chief Controller Knox, and in October, 1943, ill-health forced her to lay it down. Her mantle fell deservedly on her Deputy, Senior Controller Whateley. She, with her insight into the nature of a command of women wrote an individual letter to every officer which epitomizes leadership of the ATS and must be quoted in full:

'Dear . . .
    I am addressing this letter to all my officers, being the only method whereby I can contact you individually without further delay. I look forward, of course, to meeting you in person, but

in view of the size of our Service and the area it covers, you will, I know, understand that personal contact must, of necessity, be a slow process.

In this fifth year of war I realize how very weary many of you must be, and I think you should know that, as Director, I regard the welfare and well-being of my officers of primary importance. It is, I am sure, superfluous for me to say that the welfare and well-being of the Other Ranks is the first consideration for us all. This duty is delegated to you, but I realize that unless I have done everything possible, and I repeat possible, for my officers they cannot carry out this delegation.

It is only human nature that you serving outside should feel that we in the War Office are blind to many of the worries and anxieties, both Service and private, with which you are daily beset. To this I would reply that we (and here I speak specifically for myself) are far from blind. At this moment my thoughts and those of my staff are directed to seek the best ways and means to lighten your burdens and give you fresh hope and energy to carry on.

Without love of justice and a great human understanding no great work can succeed. I can at least assure you of both, and in conclusion ask you to believe that I am so very aware of how much your success *and* happiness depends on

Yours sincerely,
LESLIE E. WHATELEY.

Such, briefly, and with many omissions, is the story of one of the most outstanding feats of military organization in the history of the British Army. It is time now to turn and take a further look at the work the women of the organization were doing for the Army.

Chapter VI

Chronicles of Success

THE achievements of the ATS in 1943–44 were twofold. First, we must remember that in 1940 no British force existed capable of fighting a powerful enemy equipped for war in the age of technology. The army, lightly armed and organized mainly for peace-keeping in the Empire, had not abandoned horsed cavalry; there were no armoured or airborne divisions, the anti-aircraft defence of the country only existed in rudimentary form, virtually nothing was known about amphibious operations and there was no proper equipment for it; indeed we were short of modern weapons of every kind. The highly trained armies with their lavish and sophisticated equipment which won the victories of the second period of war, while the few hastily reorganized regular and territorial divisions just held the outer ring, were only built up after three years of hard work. (This is the dull side of military history, which the popular, non-professional reader skips in favour of exciting battles and disasters and defeats.) In this marvellous feat of organization the women were integrated into every branch of the supporting arms and services behind the actual firing line, and in Anti-Aircraft Command they were actually in the firing line. In this sense the history of the Auxiliary Territorial Service is part and parcel of the history of the British Army during one of the most splendid and successful phases of its long and dogged career. We are not talking about a unit, or even an ubiquitous specialist service (The REME, the QARANC and the RADC have their histories, and very interesting they are), but of some 204,000 odd military personnel who happened to be of the female sex who undertook every military task save handling lethal weapons and were located everywhere except in the combat zone where they would be at physical risk.

The other angle, and it is one to be stressed, although we are here concerned with the military and not the social history of Britain, is that the period now reached was a notable step forward in the emancipation of women. Every anti-feminist has quoted – or misquoted – at some time or another Dr Johnson's crack: 'Sir, a woman's preaching is like a dog walking on his hinded legs. It is not done well, but you are surprised to find it done at all'. This view, extended generally to all female excursions outside the kitchen, the nursery, or the sickroom, still persists in little minds here and there even today, but as the war went forward it was first eroded and by 1944 totally discredited. The only reason the work of the Army's women did not make a bigger impact is partly because in that crisis we all had other things to think about beside the rivalry between the sexes, and partly because women had become part of the military and industrial scene without any great drama. The very success of this enormous operation guaranteed its dullness or, to be correct, its *apparent* dullness.

The fact is that war is a terribly dull business – endless boredom, punctuated by moments of extreme fear, as the saying goes. Women are temperamentally fitted for some reason to endure such a state of affairs better than men, and as for moments of extreme fear the Victorian image – one wholly unjustified, if we look at what women did put up with in the way of plague, siege, mutiny and shipwreck – they proved very disappointing to their detractors. Reading the records, frustration can be sensed even among the public relations men; in moments of danger and even death the women proved as stoical as the men. As for ability, although they were not called upon to preach, they showed finally that women could carry out any task within their physical capacity as well as their brothers and, one dare say, where patience, conscientousness, deftness and attention to detail are required, a good deal better.

In air defence, for instance, it is not extreme fear that is the trouble, but the need to keep up a razor sharp alertness and the ability to put precise drills into action for week after week or month after month without becoming stale. Or, to take another example, ATS detachments were responsible for documenting, paying, issuing leave passes and travel warrants for drafts of soldiers entering and leaving the country, and also for the shore administration of the Maritime Regiment of the Royal Artillery. (For some odd reason outside the scope of this book the self-defence guns on the vessels of the Mercantile Marine were the responsibility of the Royal Artillery and not the Royal Navy.) The ATS posts were often in the most dismal areas of dismal ports, with little opportunity for relaxation even by the standards of war-time, and the women had for company only old and grumpy or younger and physically substandard soldiers condemned to boring, non-combatant routine. The work was either a frantic rush when a ship was paid off or commissioned, or a draft arrived unex-pectedly, or long dull periods of waiting for the next job. Here, as in many other activities the same comment crops up in the reports: 'They worked long hours' and 'They never complained'.

Nor all the work was dull routine. To start with, officers of either sex would agree that the most rewarding of all duties is that of a 'regimental' officer, whose task is the leadership and man- or woman-management which creates the bedrock of morale on which all military efficiency rests. This provided ample scope for women with intelligence and character. As well, there was a constant demand for well-educated and technically qualified women at all levels for tasks ranging from the unusual to the bizarre.

For instance, ninety per cent of the staff of the Army Blood Depot were ATS. They provided the trained orderlies for the medical officers, drivers for the travelling teams who visited blood donors (usually military units), and collected the raw blood, and the laboratory assistants who tested and sterilized it, prepared the plasma and bottled it. They blew the glass instruments required, prepared kits for collecting blood and for giving transfusions, packaged them and despatched them to user units.

The ATS provided eighty of the staff for a delicate operation gruesomely and inappropriately code-named TYBURN. One of the killer diseases of South-East Asia is scrub, or mite, typhus. The source of the vaccine was a large number of cotton-rats, imported specially from the United States and suitably infected. The ATS staff were responsible for the care of the animals in their cages and for the laboratory work of preparing the vaccine. Both were extremely hazardous tasks and elaborate precautions had to be scrupulously observed. It was all successfully done and 100,000 doses were prepared and despatched in time for the danger season of the disease in early 1945.

Typhus of a more familiar but equally horrible kind was the threat met by a handful of ATS in northern Syria in a now long forgotten and unrecorded incident. Syria was then under British military control. Quite suddenly a horde of Greek refugees decided to quit Turkey and cross the border into Syria near Aleppo. The RAMC sent up a team from the 43rd General Hospital supported by their medical orderlies, part of which set up an aid post at the crossing point, while an ATS sergeant and five more orderlies established a disinfestation post in the only accommodation they could find, which was a disused 1914 Turkish military barracks. A few days' hard scrubbing, copious disinfectant and some paint put the place in order in time for an influx of refugees at the rate of 1,000–1,500 a day who were, as such unfortunate people often are, unmanageable, hysterical, complaining and mostly lousy (body lice, of course being the typhus vector). The auxiliaries took them firmly in hand, persuading everyone under their care, 'from tiny babies to the oldest crones', to strip for medical inspection and to have their clothes taken away and be disinfested in the special apparatus brought up for the purpose.

Aleppo was well off the tourist beat (and still is) but the chance to explore an unspoiled Asian city was frustrated by the friendly but astonished citizens who had seen very few European ladies, let alone women 'soldiers' in uniform, and surrounded the girls or followed them in crowds, waiting outside shops until they came out, until they gave up sight-seeing in despair.

The ATS team put in to supervise all the domestic arrangements for the VIPs attending the Cairo conference of 1943 had an equally unusual but pleasanter task, seeing great men at close quarters and winning golden opinions from everyone. The sergeant responsible for the villa where Chiang Kai-shek and his famous wife were lodged was rewarded in a more solid form—a gold watch as a memento.

The ATS supported the Royal Engineers in a number of ways. The Sappers were responsible for the theory of camouflage and artists were required at the Camouflage School, from which many ingenious ideas and much good advice emerged.

The works service required architectural draughtsmen; in fact, draughtswomen were employed by the RE, the RASC, the RAOC, the REME and by the Military College of Science, where diagrams of all the new munitions coming into service were required for instruction. The most important contribution made in this field was in the production of up-to-date maps. We forget in peacetime training carried out in familiar training areas and field-firing ranges the enormous appetite a modern army has for maps, mainly of 1:50,000 or the familiar One inch to One Mile. Every tank commander, every platoon commander and his sergeant, every artillery officer and his assistants, to start at the lowest level, requires not only the map sheets covering his immediate operational area but sufficient to allow for the rapid moves of modern mobile warfare. Gridded maps are the only accurate way of describing locations, they are required for all tactical planning, and without maps close air support and artillery and mortar fire control is almost impossible. No such supply of maps existed, and further-more operational maps have to be dead up-to-date and containing trigonometrical data for the engineers and artillery. In war orders for basic maps could hardly be placed in foreign bookshops nor could survey teams be sent off in advance to future operational theatres. Some areas in Asia were only sketchily mapped or not mapped at all. The basic topographical data was obtained by the RAF photographical squadrons after many laborious and some-times dangerous sorties and correlated with information from intelligence sources. From this, the Royal Engineers, supported by five ATS Drawing Sections with seventy-three tradeswomen prepared the large-scale master sheets, drawn and coloured by hand, from which the millions of maps required were produced.

Military administration demands the movement of large numbers of documents whose contents either clog the communications or the postal service. The ATS was fully committed to the Microgram Service, in which documents were microphotographed so that one hundred feet of film could carry 1,600 pages of type, which were reprocessed at the rate of 1,000 an hour on receipt and despatched to their addresses.

The ATS was also involved in photography, film making and film projection, which became increasingly important as a training aid for the expanding armies. Their training took eight weeks, four in the theory of electricity, sound and optics, plus some elementary circuitry and maintenance followed by a month's experience in a civilian cinema. Sixty-five operators were required for the Dome Trainer, an early but very ingenious and effective device for training the layers of light anti-aircraft gunners without using live ammunition. (A projector threw the picture of a real aircraft, making realistic noises, on to the inside of a large dome representing the sky, and the shot from the dummy gun was represented by a spot of light.)

Making training films of all kinds became virtually an industry which was later extended into propaganda films. The ATS assisted in scripting, cutting, joining and editing. They were involved in, among other successes, the preparation of the film *Desert Victory*.

The Royal Artillery had an insatiable appetite for skilled operators of one kind and another. Apart from the ATS element of Anti-Aircraft Command, which in 1943 was some 57,000 strong of which 9,671* were 'operators, Fire Control, AA, a 'trade', the Gunners employed skilled staff for testing new weapons. The officers had to have an appropriate science degree, and the NCOs and auxiliaries a basic knowledge of physics and mathematics to about the present 'O' level. The work was healthy, but hard,

---

* All the figures in this chapter are taken from the 30 September, 1943, strength return which represents peak total strength of the ATS in the war.

involving long sessions using instruments to record the fall of shot in the open in all weathers, followed by laborious calculations of the results using pencils, tables and paper, there being then no computers or pocket calculating machines. Apropos of this work there is an interesting picture of Dame Helen Gwynne-Vaughan when DATS inspecting the ATS staff at the Proof and Experimental Establishment at Shoeburyness. The auxiliaries are wearing greatcoats and what are unmistakably the red and blue Royal Artillery forage caps ('side-hats', worn fore and aft), not the soft ATS peaked cap, and the officer is wearing the range uniform of the Establishment, a side-hat, blue reefer jacket and a white skirt to match the white duck trousers of the male staff. The excuse for this exclusive and traditional rig is that the range staff are responsible for firing safety and entry to the impact area to recover test projectiles, and that they must be easily distinguished, because the officer in charge's orders are overriding, regardless of rank and must be obeyed immediately. It was a tribute to the ATS to be admitted to this jealous fraternity and pleasant to record that (as far as is known) the practice was unimpeded by any fussy insistence on ATS clothing regulations. (It is a feature of the British army as compared with all others that every unit will, if possible, try to wear something *outré* and distinct from anything worn by anyone else. 'Uniform' is something it avoids wearing at all cost.)

When invasion threatened, the coast artillery of the old harbour defence systems was greatly expanded and after the threat of invasion had subsided was kept in being, for had the enemy been sufficiently enterprising they could have launched raids on the long coastline of Britain which would have been damaging to public morale, and a most definite threat to the increasingly congested assembly areas where the invasion forces were being built up in 1944. As well as the usual administrative support, the ATS provided 137 operators for the coast defence plotting rooms which kept track of all shipping moving in the coastal shipping lanes.

Other activities remain cloaked in the obscurity of the 'miscellaneous' column of the returns, and include the women working in the intelligence agencies, whose numbers were small but whose work was important. (The ATS was not involved in clandestine or behind-the-lines activities.)

Mid-1941 saw a completely fresh departure. The task of ATS officers was almost entirely concerned with the discipline and welfare of the rank and file, who provided the technical support for the army in the appropriate trades. But this was a system which did not fully exploit the officer's capabilities. A manpower comb-out found some 800 fit young male officers employed on the staff in static headquarters whose place could be taken by officers in the ATS, so women were duly selected and trained in 'A' and 'Q' staff duties. The first staff course of twelve weeks was held in the autumn at the School of Military Administration, after which two were held at the short-lived ATS Staff College and then seven at the ATS wing of the Staff College itself. The eleventh course took place at the Junior Staff College just after the war ended.

The ATS also provided a few highly trained 'staff secretaries' for senior commanders and chiefs of staff, ranging in rank from junior commander to warrant officer. So we see how in five short but eventful years after the whole idea of a women's service in uniform had been turned down flat, the Army had come round to recognizing its possibilities.

The odd tasks and occupations described above illustrate the versatility of the Service, but to convey a full picture it is necessary to resort to statistics, split down to arms and services, and then see what the various contingents were doing. Taking September, 1943, as the median point, the total strength at home was 207,398 and 5,077 overseas, 5,000 of these concentrated in the Middle East Command. Later this figure began to go down, partly because the fraction required to train the ATS force itself could be reduced after peak strength was reached, partly because of natural wastage as the four-year engagements ran out, partly because the enemy air threat was reduced as more and more of the Channel Coast was cleared, but mainly for the reason that national priorities demanded that female labour had to be diverted to industry or to produce food on the land. In June, 1945, when demobilization had already started the total effectives were 184,190. It is worth noting, and

7

flattering to the Service, that when recruiting was cut down sharply the Army was calling for a ceiling of 200,000 in the static chain and the Gunners could have accepted up to 100,000 in AA Command.

Of the total strength around 24,000 was required to run the administrative and training machine, which had in it some 6,300 trainees in the pipe-line. Of the major users AA Command employed 56,178 women, a figure roughly equivalent to seventy battalions of infantry or the fighting element of either the Eighth or the Fourteenth Armies. Women exceeded men in AA Command, and constituted the main labour force—15,260—in the static communication network operated by the Royal Corps of Signals. The Royal Army Pay Corps with 11,188 was also dependent almost entirely on a woman's service to keep going as far as the main pay and records offices were concerned. After the Gunners the biggest employers were the RAOC with 22,648 and the RASC with 17,013. There were 6,208 in the REME. If these are taken in turn it will be seen how far the utilization of woman-power had progressed from the humble but useful stage of orderlies, typists, cooks and batwomen to the skilled army trades.

The Royal Corps of Signals in addition to its responsibilities for communications within the armies in the field operated a world-wide chain of static communications which connected the War Office with theatre headquarters abroad and Commands and static establishments at home. Under its supervision the ATS operated the telephone, teleprinter, telegraph and radio services at the receiving and despatching ends, and provided a sizeable proportion of the despatch rider letter service. They provided 10,588 tradeswomen of one kind and another: 3,458 teleprinter operators, 3,972 telephone switchboard operators (later a general trade called 'operator, line, wireless and key' was introduced, which was more highly skilled and allowed a flexible deployment), 1,071 miscellaneous Royal Signals trades and 1,087 potential tradeswomen learning on the job.

The heart of the system was the underground signal centre in the War Office where 30,000 messages a week were cleared. The

ATS manned the long double bank of teleprinters and the switch-boards in two shifts of seven hours and a night shift, when the traffic was less intense, of ten hours. After D-Day the teleprinter network was extended to Normandy. The ATS manned the signal centre at General Eisenhower's headquarters and the task of receiving, registering, routing and transmitting his historic signal reporting that OVERLORD, the invasion of Nazi-held France had begun, fell to seven auxiliaries.

The ATS was also responsible for preparing the punched tapes on which were coded the messages for the high-speed radio transmitters which connected the Office with theatres overseas.

The postal services in the British Army are the responsibility of the Royal Engineers, who employed 1,500 ATS as sorters and in other duties, who worked eight-hour shifts and handled 8,000 letters a day. Regular mail is for soldiers in the field not simply an adjunct to 'welfare', it is essential to morale, and the ATS made a substantial contribution to the work of the Army Post Office which somehow, in all the difficulties of world-wide war, delivered letters to the far-ranging armoured columns in the Western Desert, the infantry edging forward in the cold, wet mountains of Italy and the Chindit columns marching deep in the jungles of Burma behind the enemy lines. Very often soldiers and their families lost touch, through the accidents of war, cross-posting, being admitted to hospitals or sometimes simply through failing to write or not telling their families their new addresses. The ATS ran a bureau for dealing with enquiries from anxious wives or parents and re-establishing contact. Another office had the delicate and often sad task dealing with returned undelivered letters, taking great care to hold them back until they had found out the fate of the addressee and if he had died or was a prisoner of war or had been killed, so as to ensure that his next of kin had received the official notification before the letters were returned.

The RASC, whose association with the FANY and the ATS went back to their earliest days, employed 17,013 at home, including 4,606 tradeswomen among whom there were 336 driver mechanics and 516 storewomen. The RASC employed 6,608 ordinary drivers – 'Drivers, IC' – almost half the global total. As well there were 277 drivers in the Middle East, and a solitary one in East Africa. As the war went on these figures altered substantially and the services of ATS drivers for motor ambulance companies and general transport were expanded in the major overseas theatres as will be described in a later chapter.

Transport is one of the most precious commodities in war and every unit and individual jealously claimed the right to the exclusive service of a unit or, preferably, his own private vehicle. This led to waste and poor maintenance, so in 1942 all transport not specifically on the establishment of an operational unit and essential for its functioning was grouped into RASC Command Mixed Transport Companies, RASC or ATS filling posts in the stores, garages and headquarters, with transport platoons either all ATS under ATS officers, or all RASC, the number of platoons being varied to meet the load.

At the same time the boundaries between the work of the RASC and the RAOC were also redrawn in the interests of rationalization. Traditionally the RASC, which had pioneered the use of motor transport in the British Army had been so far responsible for procuring its own vehicles and for their repair and maintenance, while the RAOC catered for the rest of the Army. Repairs were to become the province of the Royal Electrical and Mechanical Engineers, a new corps, which relieved the RAOC of that responsibility, but at the same time it assumed the task of providing the RASC with its vehicles, which added to its main burden of providing warlike stores and vehicles for the expanding armies at home and abroad. All the vast array of new equipment, all the guns, tanks and 'warlike' stores of every kind from bootlaces and web equipment to millions of rounds of ammunition had to be received from whatever source it was obtained, checked for serviceability and either issued on the correct scale to the new units or stored ready for issue on demand in the RAOC depots.

Equipping the new formations and re-equipping the ones already in action with up-to-date vehicles and weapons was a prodigious task, done against time, for which the necessary machinery had to be created at the same time as the operation went forward. In some regimental histories and memoirs there are bitter comments about lorries arriving without the right tools and tanks whose radios were out of order and so on. Looking back at the magnitude of the task and all the obstacles it seems surprising that these mistakes were confined to the early part of the war and that there were so few of them. At the starting point of the operation a few regulars and reservists and the peacetime Territorials had to train a small army of men and women who had no very clear idea of the difference between a voucher and an indent, let alone look after dangerous bits of equipment like artillery fuses and explosives, or waterproof a vehicle for an amphibious landing. Altogether the RAOC employed 22,648 ATS, of whom 18,199 were tradeswomen: 6,212 were specialist 'clerks, RAOC', and 9,855 were trade-trained storewomen. Among the non-tradeswomen there were 294 ordinary storewomen and 1,983 drivers.

It is difficult to single out any particular activity, because the history of the ATS in support of the RAOC is essentially part of the history of that corps, but it would be fair to mention as an example of ATS versatility the team occupied in reconditioning ammunition. A round of modern artillery ammunition is a complicated affair, and requires careful maintenance if it is to remain serviceable, and if neglected or badly stored becomes unsafe to use. Ammunition is also extremely expensive and used in immense quantities. (The cost in money of munitions can only be notional, but Gunner officers in training were continually reminded that each round of 25 pounder ammunition cost £25, which was easy to remember and not too wide of the mark.) Unserviceable ammunition salvaged from dumps and sometimes from the flooded holds of ships was collected for the attention of the RAOC, and one of the reconditioning teams was provided by the ATS commanded by an ATS officer only 20 years old who was the only qualified female ammunition officer in the Army. Under her direction many thousands of pounds worth of ammunition was reconditioned, which involved inspecting all the components which go to make up the projectile and the cartridge – the fuses, gaines, high explosive fillings, propellants, primers – repainting the shells in their correct code colours, and repackaging them.

Closely allied to the RAOC was the new corps, the REME, who employed a much smaller contingent: 6,208 altogether, but of these 2,643 belonged to skilled trades into which in peacetime males would only be admitted after long training and in some cases apprenticeship. Among the tradeswomen appearing in the 1943 return we find radio-mechanics, motor-mechanics, welders, turners, tinsmiths, metal-machinists, fitters of various kinds, electricians, draughtswomen (for machine drawings) and coach trimmers. There was no question of the women not possessing the necessary aptitude, but this programme ran into a snag which had bedevilled the women's services throughout: wastage. Wastage tended to be high for two reasons. The first was discharge on compassionate grounds. For men the rules were fairly strict, but, without going into the ramifications of a difficult human problem, the deprivation of a daughter or sister or daughter-in-law, for many families handicapped by age, infirmity or illness and who had already been deprived of their male support, was in a different category. When in doubt it seems as if the decision was to permit release, until time and experience finally enabled the system to be tightened up without becoming harsh. The other cause was marriage, followed by the arrival of a child. (For the record it might be added here that the rate of illegitimate pregnancy was very low, at most $2\frac{1}{2}$ per cent of the rate of pregnancy in wedlock, and substantially lower than the corresponding rate in civil life at the time.) Trade training was expensive in time and effort, and if the useful period of service was curtailed it became wasteful to train women. Moreover, after 1943 it was decided as a matter of national policy that large scale recruiting for the ATS would cease and industry would have priority. Many trained women remained to soldier on, but after 1944 training for all REME trades was discontinued.

A statistical enquiry into the deployment of the ATS could be continued at great length and in great detail, but it is sufficient to say here that the ATS were represented in every arm and service, including the headquarters and training units of the combat arms; 4,544 with the infantry, for example, and a modest 64 with the short-lived Reconnaissance Corps. It was to provide cooks that the original operation under the initiative of the Women's Legion had started. It is certainly worth recording that 27 years later from the modest beginnings by the dogged 'ladies with the frying-pan', this side of the women's work had grown to 2,237 tradeswomen cooks, of which 29 were 'cooks, hospital', 18,555 ordinary unit-trained cooks and 3,183 learner cooks; a total of 23,975.

This is a suitable moment to discuss the administrative machine which made all this possible, whose organization was described in the previous chapter. There was a minority opinion, and not entirely a male one, that complete integration would have been more economical, i.e. that the women could have been slotted in to the unit establishments as appropriate, belonged in every sense to the regiment, arm or service concerned and have been looked after in all respects exactly as the men were, by their officers, and so save a great deal of overheads. The Army dislikes dual control or dual command, anyway, and there always were—and will be—inevitable arguments and struggles for power about the 'ownership' of units in formation with mixed cap badges. This minority view never made any headway. The senior commanders and staff officers concerned had no doubts whatever on the subject of the existing ATS command and advisory structure. Politically integration was not possible. As the investigations of the Markham Committee and the subsequent close attention given by Press and Members of Parliament showed, the nation was determined that its daughters—and remember that the majority of them were very young—should be cared for by women in what was for them initially a strange and alarming environment.

Violet Markham put the case succinctly in a correspondence she had with the commanding officer of one of the mixed heavy anti-aircraft regiments. 'Women in the services' (she said) 'raise a good many problems and as an onlooker I am interested in the very sharp division of opinion about control and management—whether there should be complete integration or whether the women should remain, for some purposes, entirely under their own women officers . . .'

'I know that many officers share your view that the women should be wholly under the men's direction, and from the logical and theoretical point of view there is a great deal to be said for it. Life, however, is not ruled by logic and I think you must remember that when women are forming part of a fighting service they are doing something quite abnormal, and the adjustments must, in any case, be difficult. Parliament and public opinion would, I am sure, not agree to the authority of the women officers being wholly superseded. I hear both sides of this argument very frequently and appreciate the strength of each position, but I think somehow you will have to work out a middle path, and must accept with good temper and patience the rough edges which will always exist. So much depends on the personal factor. I feel sure from the way you write that an officer like yourself might safely be entrusted with the welfare of girls. There are other officers of whom one could not say that with equal certainty, and others who would be more susceptible to the feminine appeal of a bit of fluff than any women would be! On the whole, I think that a woman's judgment of another woman is better than that of a man, and some of the WAAF,* where integration is much more complete than the ATS, agree with me about this.'

The cost in womanpower of the administrative machine was not a light one: the question is whether it was excessive. The figures are all available, but as in all such questions they are difficult to evaluate. For instance, it employed 255 ATS cooks, who would have been cooking for the ATS however they were deployed and the same can be said of the 20 'tailoresses', the chiropodists, the PT instructresses and the hairdressers.

It was essential to an ATS equivalent of the military police to carry out normal provost duties; that is, keeping an eye on dress and discipline in public places, and assisting at railway stations with information concerning time-tables, routes, auxiliaries travel-

* The Women's Auxiliary Air Force, now the Women's Royal Air Force.

ling on duty stranded without transport, or who had missed trains and were technically absent or required temporary accommodation. In January, 1942, the provost branch of the ATS was started. Training was at the Corps of Military Police depot at Mychett, and in 1943 their strength was 752 counting only those in Home Forces.

The total of administrative staff and the permanent staff in the ATS schools and training units was 24,121, which is the worst case, because it can be argued that the women would have had to have basic training whether integrated or not. Crediting the trainees in the pipe-line to the effective work force, it appears that 88½ per cent of the ATS were profitably employed. This would be a satisfactory figure judged by the standard of any military organization. Admittedly it was a far cry from the private flat in London staffed by two energetic ladies ordering uniforms from Selfridges and sending round to the local Labour Exchange for recruits, but starting from the impetus given by Dame Helen and her ruthless insistence on efficiency and correct 'staff duties' the Directors and Controllers had created from scratch an organization of which the General Staff or the management of any great industrial concern would have been proud.

The proof of the pudding was in the eating. There was occasional carping. During Operation DIVER, for instance, when AA Command rapidly deployed southwards to counter the V-weapon, conditions on the gun positions were very rough and many girls were in tents amid the mud roughing it along with the male Gunners, but they were not particularly grateful to an ex-Beaverbrook journalist, Tom Driberg, MP (later Lord Bradwell) for 'exposing' the conditions under which they were working. Generally, after the publication of the Markham Report and the hard work by Directors Jean Knox and Leslie Whateley there were no chinks to be found in the administrative armour and the morale and conduct of the Service world-wide was unassailable. The real purpose of the organization was the maintenance of morale, and the work of improving welfare, or to use the preferred ATS term, 'well-being', constantly pressed ahead.

Surely it was very advanced in 1944 to engage three sociologists or social scientists with good academic qualifications and practical experience to advise the ATS staff on problems of personnel management, give lectures and provide counsel for units on their especial problems? On the spiritual side the Churches Committee for Work among Women in H.M. Forces provided 'chaplain's assistants', who did much good work in organizing religious services, assisting in confirmation classes, giving individual counsel where it was required and supporting the regular chaplains, of whom there were never enough. The Markham Report had made the important point that arrangements for well-being should cater for the mind as well as for material comfort. This took three forms. A certain amount of formal education was provided for those who wished to prepare themselves for demobilization and wished to exercise their minds, run by the Royal Army Education Corps and attached ATS officers. Then there was recreational education in such subjects as handicrafts, gramophone concerts of classical music, play readings and amateur theatricals. As well it was the Army's policy to educate all ranks in the purpose of the war and the nature of the society they were trying to defend, by means of the programmes run by the Army Bureau of Current Affairs and 'The British Way and Purpose' leaflets.

Here certain difficulties were met, some of them common to male and female units. In operational units in AA command where there was an established training routine such activities were regarded as training and duly included in the weekly programmes by which the soldiers were kept profitably busy between air raids. In the static establishments which worked long industrial hours, usually with a back-log of work, there was a good deal of obstruction, and such things as physical training periods, 'padrés hours', domestic 'make and mend' periods in barracks and recreational or educational periods had to come out of the girl's spare time and were unpopular. (PT was *always* unpopular, and there was a running battle about it throughout the war, not least because shortage of clothing prevented the issue of suitable PT dress.)

The ABCA discussions were met with what one of the official

reports calls 'a wall of dumbness'. The trouble was that the political awareness of the girls and their general knowledge was low, and it was very difficult to get them interested. (The same can be said of the great majority of their male comrades.) The junior officers, on whom the main burden of running the educational classes fell, were little better. Instruction was based on discussion and drawing out the tongue-tied is a skill acquired only with difficulty by university tutors and staff college instructors. Discussions were, therefore, sticky and as for lectures all soldiers are experts at not listening to them while maintaining an air of wooden attention. In consequence a lot of this praiseworthy effort simply washed over the majority of the women, as it did the men, but it was worth doing. Someone no doubt will attempt a study of the post-war social consequences of the educational programme to which a large segment of the young women of the country were exposed for two or three years. Some of it must have stuck.

However, this is a digression, although an important one. As 1944 wore on, great events pushed all such side-issues into the background. A great part of AA Command redeployed and went into continuous action against the new threat of the 'flying bombs', or 'cruise missiles', as we would call them today. The work of the services reached the climax they had been aiming at for the whole war: the readying of the invasion armies for crossing the Channel.

Peak strength was one measure of the ATS achievement. Peak effort, which culminated in D-Day and OVERLORD was another. No one who was not alive and in Britain in 1944 can enter into the feelings of emotion with which the news of the invasion was heard. 1941 and the first nine months of 1942 had been years of nothing but bad news. In 1943 things began to look up, and for those who could take the long view the Russian victories, the clearing of the coast of North Africa and the Allied landings in Italy all showed that the tide had turned in our favour, but as long as the Germans were ensconced along the Channel coast the British people felt hemmed in. 'D-Day' is simply a staff term and there had already been 'D-Days' in the Mediterranean, but *the* D-Day – the dawn of liberation and the sure sign that the war was really going to end –

was 6 June, 1944. It was to this end that every administrative nerve was strained and the ATS made their greatest combined effort. It would be otiose to recite another long catalogue of their activities. It is enough to say that all are agreed that without the women's task force the thing could not have been done. On the night of the 5 June two senior ATS officers in the south of England were returning from an inspection and heard the roar of countless aircraft passing overhead. Security was tight; but they guessed that this was 'the real thing' at last. It was the airborne divisions who were to be the spearheads on their way.

Early next morning Lance-Corporal Parry, ATS, on duty in the SHAEF signal office was handed the laconic message:

'Under command of General Eisenhower, Allied naval forces, supported by strong air forces, began landing Allied armies this morning on the northern coasts of France', and the news was broadcast to Britain and the world.

Chapter VII

Service Overseas

As we have seen an army of 207,000 women was hard at work in Home Forces by the end of 1943, but demands for ATS support were soon coming in from every theatre, especially from the Middle East. It is worth noting that the ATS never had to seek a role, or force the value of their support on the army as a whole, but that its leaders had perpetually to struggle to keep up with the demand. There was a substantial response to the requirements of the three major theatres – the Middle East, the Central Mediterranean and North-west Europe – and small contributions made in peripheral commands ranging from East Africa to Canada. Between 400 and 500 were employed in Washington and, in 1945, over 200 in India. (All these figures fluctuated, of course.) Although the main operations were in succession – the clearing of the Axis from Africa, the campaign in Italy and then 'D-Day' – it will be simpler to give an account of each theatre in turn up to the end of the war.

The Middle East

It will be remembered that Senior Commander Chitty had made an abortive visit to Cairo in July, 1940, but that in the November of that year the policy of not employing ATS was reversed in favour of the sensitive and secluded Combined Services Detailed Interrogation Centre where there was a requirement for a completely British-born domestic staff and the need for some absolutely secure signals operators for some secret work. The nucleus of forty-seven ATS at the CSDIC became 501 Company, ATS. The feeling in GHQ Middle East Forces about full-scale use of ATS in the command was ambivalent.

Innate military conservatism and an understandable anxiety about the difficulties of accommodating women in a strange and potentially hostile local environment, and who might also be exposed to enemy action by the swing of the battle or, worse, to falling into enemy hands militated against the use of ATS. At the same time the staff never ceased to be worried by the civilian status of the very large number of females who worked in almost every department and wanted badly to bring them under military law.

The most GHQ were able to do in this respect — the specific reasons for picking on this particular unit are now lost in time — was to insist on No. 11 Unit, Motor Transport Corps established, or recognized, in February, 1941, converting to ATS. (The MTC was an autonomous, uniformed, voluntary, quasi-military body, and like the FANY socially somewhat selective in its recruiting.) Half the ladies agreed to enrol; the other half were sent back to England. The new unit became 502 Ambulance Car Company and earned a well-deserved reputation for efficiency. It re-equipped in Helmieh in November, 1941, with thirty-two ambulances, a three-tonner, two utility trucks and a motorcycle, and then moved up to Alexandria where it came under the DDMS of 16 Area and served the 8th and 64th General hospitals. 502 was kept busy during the hard fighting of 1942. In October and November of that year it evacuated many of the wounded of the famous 9th Australian Division, and later, when the tide of battle had finally run westwards, operated along the Eighth Army's line of communication by detachments from Mersah Matruh back as far as Cairo. The company earned one MBE and six mentions in despatches. Then followed a less exciting period when the company suffered that indignity resented by all efficient units (which often and unavoidably happened), the order to surrender their flawlessly maintained vehicles for reissue to an active theatre and to receive some rubbish in return. An upturn in their fortunes took place in 1944, when the company was again re-equipped and redeployed in Italy, complete with their mysterious unit sign, 'a blue devil facing right on a white background', and their cherished mascot, Pandora the poodle bitch.

The company retained a very strong *esprit de corps* until the end of the war. When its members volunteered to enrol in the ATS they agreed on condition that the original MTC members would not be dispersed by casual posting, and this was duly honoured. So was a promise made to Junior Commander Otto, who was promoted to command the whole of the Alexandria Group of ATS units. There she could keep in touch with her former comrades, but she asked that if 502 Company was moved to another theatre she might be allowed to revert in rank so as to resume command and go with it. This was also agreed and duly honoured. As it happened the Alexandria group was disbanded about the same time as the ATS in the command were reorganized. This was wise and showed the good sense of the ATS commanders concerned. *Esprit de corps* is the basis of all military efficiency; it takes root with difficulty and can be demolished by a single tactless move. In 1945 when there was a shortage of officers the Assistant Director ATS in Italy, Chief Commander M. Baker, appealed to the Company, whose members were almost all potential officers, to apply for commissions, but all but a few refused. They had been together for over four years and preferred to see the war out as a team.

Senior Commander Chitty returned to MEF (Middle East Forces) in November, 1941, to assume the post of Assistant Director ATS and the rank of Controller in January, 1942. Her mission was to see whether it was possible to raise a sufficiently strong force of ATS by local recruiting, an operation which was politically the hottest of potatoes and fraught with every kind of difficulty. Fortunately the British companies, 501 and 502, were very busy and fully capable of looking after themselves, so the newly established ADATS was able to concentrate on her main aim. (Like other ATS they found that one of the blessings of serving overseas was the freedom to get on with the job unhampered by the endless and jealous scrutiny of the public and press. There was no question that their well-being was in any way neglected but, the blitz apart, the ATS in the war theatres were shorter of amenities than the women at home, put up with unpleasant conditions in the war theatres, and sometimes lived in as rugged conditions as their male comrades when they had to without complaining. Egypt and the central Mediterranean are not all blue skies and sunny beaches: one can be frozen, drenched, choked by a sandstorm or suffocated by a khamsin according to the time and place.)

The chief demand in Egypt and Palestine was for drivers, general duty women, nursing orderlies, and storewomen for the great ordnance and supply depots at Tel-el-Kebir in particular. Commander Chitty's plan was admirably sound and simple, and also completely successful, and while the ATS would certainly admit that the efficient administration staff in the theatre gave every assistance, hers was a display of managerial skill of which any civil or military staff could be proud. Essentially, she had to set up shop without delay, collect and train a cadre of officers and NCOs to command the new companies as they formed, and then recruit, train and feed in a flow of auxiliaries who could be deployed as the staff demanded. Senior Commander M. H. Pine and Junior Commander K. Stocker and eight NCOs arrived from England on 11 January, followed by six more officers and 52 NCOs, to form the training staff or to take command of ATS detachments and units as they were formed. The Middle East ATS Training Centre was created in January, 1942 out of a job lot of unfinished buildings, huts, tents and field ablutions at Sarafand, which was later extended to accommodate the Middle East Officer Cadet Training Unit, in March. Later a Driver Training Wing was set up in Egypt and, in 1943, a small ATS TC, in Limassol in Cyprus. Officer selection was at first *ad hoc* and by interview, but as things became sorted out Controller Chitty formed a proper selection unit run on the same lines as in Home Forces and drawn from her senior officers. The ATS staff wasted no time in grappling with the business of making the training centre habitable and at the same time drawing up training programmes for a polyglot intake of girls, some without English,

16　WRAC driver with male colleagues in Germany

17　WRAC officer instructs recruits in military tactics

18 WRAC kennel maid

19 Combined operations at a motor rally

some very bright, some illiterate and all with differences of language, culture and temperament. There was no *lingua franca* in the Middle East apart from sometimes imperfect English, and instruction seems to have been miraculously carried on through interpreters and with the help of the locally enlisted bi-lingual women as they passed through the OCTU.

Commander Chitty, with no help except from Second Subaltern M. Chapman (who had served briefly in the ATS in Home Forces but had been returned to Rhodesia on compassionate grounds and now returned to the Service), decided that the field promising the quickest results for recruiting was Palestine, where the women of the Jewish community of settlers and refugees from Europe had the necessary intelligence, education and motivation to join in the struggle against the Nazis. The political situation was thorny, to say the least. The British as the mandatory power had to maintain an even balance of favour between Arab and Zionists and although the prospect of recruiting more than a few Christian Arabs, due to the Muslim attitude to women, was remote, the faintest shade of partiality could be pounced on as a grievance by either side, who had been at war in 1939. The Jewish desire to make an all Jewish armed contribution to the Allied effort was viewed with deep suspicion.

Controller Chitty was far from blind to the Zionist attitude and the Jewish determination to extract political advantage whenever possible and, as a matter of protocol, made her first approach to Lady MacMichael, who was local commandant of the Red Cross to whom the Palestine Auxiliary Nursing Volunteers (PANV) were affiliated. She had hoped that some members from PANV might be persuaded to come across to the ATS and provide a nucleus of officers and NCOs for command. Controller Chitty soon found that Lady MacMichael had perceived that every move the Jewish community made was motivated by self-interest and the possible advantages likely to accrue in the post-war situation, and was nervous about the consequences of commissioning Jewish girls or allowing the locally recruited ATS to be dominated by one group. The British appreciation

8

of Jewish attitudes was perfectly correct, but as far as the armed forces were concerned it was irrelevant to the war effort. Twelve girls from PANV were recommended for training, but Controller Chitty was tipped off that she would get nowhere without the assistance of Mrs Samuel of the Jewish Agency and also of the Council of Jewish Women's Organizations in Palestine, a woman of great influence. She therefore had to move with consummate tact, which was not on the face of it compatible with the speed with which she wished to act. Somehow she managed it, with diplomacy a professional might have envied.

She soon succeeded in establishing a warm rapport with Mrs Samuel, who in her turn proved a good friend and ally, but also a hard bargainer and up to every trick. She fought hard for the same rate of pay for the 'PATS', as the Palestine ATS came to be known, as the incoming British ATS, and lost; she argued for Hebrew as the basic language for communication, and lost; she scored a trick by issuing posters adorned with the six-pointed Star of David—which of course conveyed to other groups that the new force was to be exclusively Jewish, and she pressed for all-Jewish units with only limited and belated success. Later, as the numbers of ATS expanded there was political pressure (not only, it must be said, from the Jews) to favour certain individual women for commissions which was firmly resisted. None of this deflected Controller Chitty from the aim of creating an efficient and as far as possible an apolitical service; nor did she allow any of it to spoil her vital relationship with Mrs Samuel, who on her side bore no resentment and regarded these manoeuvres as all part of the political game. As the companies became established Mrs Samuel was invited to visit them and was duly impressed with attention paid by the British officers to their well-being.

It must be recorded that all the foreign enlisted ATS, Jews and the others, whatever their loyalties, and they were very strong, placed them second to the cause for which they were in their way fighting and their *esprit de corps* during their unblemished war service was wholly admirable. That this was achieved by a group of women who from Controller down to the British-born NCOs were largely unfamiliar with the tricky politics of the Middle East, and to whom the language and culture of the various groups were at first quite unfamiliar, was a remarkable achievement.

Controller Chitty began recruiting with a series of speeches at meetings organized by Mrs Samuel, while Second Subaltern Chapman began on a more personal basis in the orthodox way at Tel Aviv. Two other ATS officers began work at Jerusalem and Haifa as soon as they could be briefed after arrival.

The first cadre assembled in Sarafand towards the end of January, after some delays and hitches over vetting for security. (The security procedures were vexatious but necessary. Apart from the rivalry between the communities and British suspicions about the activities of some of the more extreme partisans, the Middle East contained refugees from the Balkans and all over central Europe, including Germany. It was wide open to Axis penetration and screening was essential.) This vital first course was finally made up of forty-five Jewish girls and four Christian Arabs. It ended on 1 March, when four girls proved outstanding and were commissioned immediately, and twenty-one were appointed sergeants and corporals. The remainder were sent off to 502 Company, where one or two proved able to learn to drive and the rest were employed in general duties, nearly all settling down well in spite of some initial disappointment at not having made the grade.

Recruiting of other groups followed at intervals, the wife of the Polish chargé d'affaires in Cairo setting an example by undergoing the basic training course at Sarafand herself. Eventually the language groups enlisted came to include Hebrew, Polish, Czech, Serbo–Croat (the Yugoslavs), Arabic and Greek, there being a strong Greek colony in Alexandria, as distinct from the Greek-speaking Cypriots who were recruited later. The first basic training course began on 21 March, so it will be seen that Controller Chitty and her staff had not allowed any grass to grow under their feet. The output was trained on the job in the units to which they were posted until, as said, the crying need for drivers led to the ATS organizing their own training. To run ahead of events, the median 30 September, 1943, strength state already used shows 4,511 rank and file distributed in seventeen trades and eleven occupations, with switchboard operators, nursing orderlies, drivers IC and storewomen in the majority. Of the 245 officers, a useful number, including two of the earliest commissioned 'PATS' filled staff captains' and equivalent appointments. The maximum strength in the Middle East was 300 officers and 4,834 NCOs and auxiliaries in March, 1943, a year after the first course. After this it declined as Italy was reinforced.

In mid-summer 1942 the order of battle was as follows: (As far as it can be summarized: it was fluid and changeable and it is not now entirely clear which companies were all-British, which were mixed and which were all of one language group. Some new companies were raised and some formed by others throwing off cadres.) 501 was with the CSDIC, 502 was based in Alexandria, the new 503 was working in the vehicle parks and delivering new vehicles to field force units at a hand-over point near Mena, 504 served the great ordnance depot at Tel-el-Kebir, 505 was at Haifa, 508 was first based at Mena and then moved into the old Citadel Barracks in Cairo, and 513, an all-Palestinian car Company, was also at Mena, where it was formed from a cadre thrown off by 503. 503 in fact threw off two cadres to form new companies, under the able direction of Junior Commander J. R. Fletcher.

1942 was notable for two events, both intimately affecting the ATS. The first was the 'Great Flap', sometimes referred to as 'Ash Wednesday', from the panic burning of masses of secret files. It was caused by the shattering defeat of the Eighth Army at Gazala, the fall of Tobruk in June and the ensuing rout stemmed only at the Ruweisat Ridge on 1 July. The story of that series of battles has been told too often to require repeating here, except to remind the younger readers that for a brief space there seemed to be nothing between the Libyan frontier and Cairo able to stop the panzers crashing through to the great base and the Suez Canal. In fact, both sides were at their last gasp – Rommel was down to twenty-seven tanks altogether — but the British and Commonwealth forces under Auchinleck's leadership gasped a little longer. It is frequently the case that the farther back from the battlefield the view-point the more frightening the prospects are. The wildest rumours circulate, the tidings of disaster are embroidered and there is a feeling of doom and defencelessness, leading to panic. The *dolce vita* of Cairo was shattered by the news, masses of military documents were burnt, impossible plans for withdrawing the whole headquarters and even the ponderous base were hurriedly drawn up; there was frantic packing of stores, so the ATS records say, at Tel-el-Kebir, and the advanced ATS detachment at Kilo 4 on the Alexandria road was pulled back as if the arrival of the Afrika Korps in the neighbourhood of the Pyramids was hourly expected. (502 seems to have carried on uninterrupted much further forward at Alexandria.)

One hasty decision was to seize the opportunity to enrol all the civilian ladies working in GHQ into the ATS, nominally and quite untrained. (What useful purpose this was to serve is not now clear, because if the enemy was amenable to international law and the usages of war they would be protected either as women, civilians or camp followers, or if in uniform would presumably be treated as prisoners of war; whereas if the enemy was not, neither label nor status would protect them.) They were all required to sign enrolment forms conditionally, which would become operative if their headquarters were evacuated from Egypt, and they were issued with uniform on the same basis. The ATS, as a trained and disciplined force, understandably viewed this fictitious use of their cap badge and uniform as highly irritating. One ATS recruit, of five weeks service, when asked if she was 'emergency', replied coldly that she was a 'regular': not quite accurate but it shows how quickly the ATS *esprit de corps* took root. All turned out well in the end, the Great Flap died down as rapidly as it had arisen, to become a rich source of comical or shame-faced military anecdote, and Cairo society returned to normal. The ATS do not seem to have been unduly perturbed. Their only involvement was the subsequent labour of recovering uniforms from the sometimes tenacious fingers of the ladies now safe from conscription.

The second great event of the year was the re-organization and re-equipping of the Eighth Army, which gave the ATS, especially those working in Tel-el-Kebir, as much work as they could possibly have wanted.

The importance of the Middle East as a base did not decrease after the victory of October–November, 1942, at Alamein. If anything the opposite was the case, because the BNAF set-up in Algeria and Tunisia was never able to take its place. More, not less ATS were required to take the place of the troops who had been deployed further west. 513 Company now worked a convoy route from Beirut in Lebanon to Tripoli in Libya, over 2,000 miles, pitching camp in the desert each evening at the end of the day's run. Life, it is recorded, held no dangers but some minor irritations for women drivers. Oddly as it reads now, the ATS provost were scandalized by some convoy drivers staging at Sarafand, who entered the town in *trousers*. There was much subsequent correspondence on the need for all drivers of convoys to carry skirts for use when off duty for 'walking out'.* But the sad lot of the military police is that the more strictly they do their duty the less popular they are. These were young and possibly overzealous members of the ATS wing who began training under the (now) Royal Corps of Military Police in May, 1943. Apart from their normal provost disciplinary duties they assisted the CMP in frontier control and any investigations involving females in criminal or security cases. It was a small but effective force (twelve in September, 1943, increased later). There were few British auxiliaries and one Greek, but the majority were Palestinian and Jewish.

In March, 1943, a mixed company of Royal Signals arrived from Britain to assist in communications; this later split into two.

* Men suffered equally from such niggling. The present writer was once reminded that his officers should always wear *ties in battle*, and there was a curious order in one Area when the new bush shirts were issued: that they should be worn *inside* the trousers, which led to a correspondence worthy of 'Beachcomber'.

One of the ATS roles was helping to operate the high-speed auto-wireless system used with the Wheatsone transmitters, and another was to work the GHQ telephone switchboards, to whose efficiency, according to the records, Junior Commander K. H. Sanderson's skill and energy made a notable contribution. By December, 1943, there were altogether four ATS signal companies. (Signal operators 'various' 92, switchboard 362 and teleprinter 20, all tradeswomen, from the September, 1943, figures reveal the extent to which communications in the theatre depended on the ATS.)

When it seemed that Palestine had been fully exploited for recruiting Controller Chitty turned her attention to Cyprus. Whether this was worth the effort seems almost a churlish question, but it did, after some traumas and some amusing incidents, produce about 120 auxiliaries. The trouble was that female emancipation did not extend to the Turkish community and not much to the Greeks, and although the reception given to the ATS officers was more than cordial, the idea of women serving in uniform was upsetting to parents, and even more so to some husbands, whose wives, mendaciously asserting that they were unmarried, sought to escape from their domestic bondage. The recruiting office was beseiged by distraught parents or indignant husbands demanding their women back. The most effective protest recorded was the dumping of an infant in the porch of the office when the recruiting officer was out, which effectively secured the release of one would-be auxiliary when she confessed it was hers. The Greek Cypriots proved a handful at first, becoming easily alarmed and even hysterical at the strange environment and the inability to communicate, but eventually a Greek Cypriot successfully passed through the OCTU (Second Subaltern Feneck) and was posted as second in command to a company in which all the Greek-speaking girls were grouped together.

The language barrier was acute, but was circumvented by one means or another. The Driver Training Wing had been formed, based on 513 Company, by Junior Commander M. Mackenzie, late FANY and OC ATS Mena. She had an instructional staff of fourteen ATS and twenty-two male driving instructors, the women concentrating on classroom instruction based on the ingenious use of cutaway engines and assemblies made of salvaged wrecks from the desert. The Wing turned out some 180 ATS drivers and thirty driver mechanics, instruction being economically combined with running convoys from the Delta across the Sinai Desert to Haifa. When there were no more girls available to train Subaltern Mackenzie was handed a bunch of locally enlisted Syrian and Lebanese males, wild but willing, to train as convoy drivers for the RASC. The languages required were basic English, dumbshow, Turkish, Arabic, Greek, Romanian and Armenian. (The recruiting net seems to have been cast rather wider than Syria, although there were Armenians in Palestine, who had settled there before 1914 at the time of the Turkish massacres of that unfortunate race.) The ATS undertook the technical instruction in the classrooms and the RASC instructors the driving. This was a great success, the ATS noting jealously that the males they had trained left for their convoy exercise having proudly put up their driver's skill-at-arms not then approved for ATS! (They were, shortly afterwards.) ATS staff officers were trained in the Middle East Training Centre, where courses for staff captains and GSO 3s along the lines of those at the School of Military Administration at home were run, and by 1945 ATS captains were holding third grade appointments in many of the static headquarters. There they did well.

(It might be noted here that the Staff Colleges, like the joint Army/RAF one at Haifa, trained second-grade staff officers mainly for operational duties in combat formations and the administration and logistics were for field formations, and sketchily dealt with at that. Some male third-grade staff officers were formally taught but most learnt at the desk. The handicap for the ATS was lack of familiarity with basic military organization and procedures, so a course was essential. There were few ATS in senior grades outside the ATS's own chain of command. An exception was Senior Commander J. Cambridge, who was a secretary at the Casablanca Conference in 1943 and later held an appointment at the Canadian National Defence HQ in Ottawa.)

As the Middle East Command gradually changed over from a fully operational theatre to a base so the role of the ATS in it began to diminish and its strength to decline. There was a steady flow of reinforcements to the ATS groups building up in Italy — 502 Ambulance Car Company, as noted, the Polish ATS and the 'PATS'. At the same time recruiting began to dry up and a supply of non-military labour for the camps and depots in the shape of Italian ex-prisoners of war (some of whom in fact had agreed to collaborate before Italy ceased to side with the Axis). The CSDIC, where the first-comers to Middle Eastern scene, 501 Company, had put in a long and unbroken stint, became redundant. So did the work of the detachment of special signal operators. Some of the ATS so freed volunteered for India; others were repatriated.

With a decrease in strength and recruiting the training organization could be contracted. The Cyprus operation had been valiant and at times amusing, at others tiresome, but its yield was small, so the Training Centre at Limassol was closed down and all that was left in Cyprus was a small holding unit in Nicosia and an ATS-run leave hostel in Troodos, much appreciated by the women's services. At the end of 1944 the ATS in the Command, down to about 4,000, were re-organized into three Groups; one in the Delta, one in the Canal Zone and one in Syria–Palestine.

There was still plenty of work to do. The Provost wing were kept busy in areas where their assistance to the military police was essential, such as the control of female refugee internees of enemy nationality, internal security and frontier control. It must be understood that until questions of sovereignty could be resolved the British forces were left exercising some of the functions of government over the whole area Jordan–Syria–Lebanon–Sinai–Egypt, and conditions were not very agreeable. The populace in Egypt, and especially Cairo, were inclined to riot, the Zionists were bracing themselves for their coming struggle to establish the state of Israel, and the Jordanians ('Transjordan'), Lebanese and Syrians were politically restive. In addition there was wide-scale theft of stores, spare parts and petrol, resulting from the shortages of war, much of it from army load-carrying vehicles, and smuggling of food-stuffs from Egypt into Palestine, which was for some reason an offence, and of course was a great temptation to drivers of vehicles convoying between the two countries.

Junior Commander Mackenzie's Driver Training Wing went from one task to the next, and from strength to strength. Having disposed of the ATS learner drivers and the locally recruited drivers for the RASC, it was given the task of training British or Indian soldiers as much needed drivers from those rendered unfit for active employment by wounds or ill-health. After this its attention was turned to training more locally enlisted men for 'UNRRA' (The United Nations Relief and Rehabilitation Administration.)

The ATS effort in the Middle East was puny compared with the giant mobilization in Home Forces if only numbers are compared, just as, indeed, the Eighth Army itself was a small formation and its bitterly fought little battles mere skirmishes compared with the vast clashes between whole groups of armies in Russia and North-West Europe, but it is not the numbers that are significant but the achievement. The Middle East was a key area in British strategy, and there the ATS made its valuable contribution. When Controller Chitty handed over to Controller M. F. Wagstaff three years after taking up the post the two original companies had grown to a force of thirty-one, over and above the many detachments and the contingent of useful staff officers. By December, 1943, 3,684 out of a total strength of 4,605 were domiciled in or refugees to the Middle East and recruited and trained there, the majority being 'PATS' of the Jewish faith and the remainder being largely Polish, Greek and Greek-speaking Cypriots. The British have in their long history of warfare employed a wide variety of fighting men, drawn from the Afghan border to Fiji and the West Indies to Somaliland, but the unique feat of the

ATS was to raise a virtual women's Foreign Legion to serve under the British flag; we must also admire the young women who gave their loyalty so completely to a service run, after all, by 'foreigners' whose aspirations and customs were as strange as their language was incomprehensible, for the common cause of defeating the Axis powers.

Africa and Italy

The next theatre of war from which there was a call for ATS support was from 'CMF', or the Central Mediterranean Forces, which included North Africa from Algiers to Tunis, where the bases and headquarters set up for the Anglo-American effort remained for some time after the invasion of Italy, and the active part of the theatre in Italy itself. In January, 1944, Controller the Lady Maud Baillie was sent out to survey the situation and see what could be done. By this time the Allies were firmly lodged on the Italian mainland, where she was immediately confronted with a demand for 6,000 women. But to explain her problem, which was different from that in Home Forces and also from Controller Chitty's in the Middle East, it is first necessary to describe the command and administrative structure, which was complicated.

In the first half of 1943 the Anglo-Americans advancing from the west and the Eighth Army from the east trapped and liquidated the Axis forces in North Africa in Tunisia. The headquarters of the British First Army was then disbanded, leaving a rump called 'British North African Forces', or BNAF. This consisted of administrative units and fighting formations waiting to go over to Italy while the front there advanced and logistic support for them developed. Sicily was cleared of the enemy, Italy surrendered and detached itself from the Axis, and after the Fifth Army had made a lodgment at Salermo and the Eighth at various points in southern Italy the line-up was: the Fifth Army— basically American, with British and French formations under command—on the left or western side of the front, and the

Eighth—British, Indian, Polish, New Zealand—on the right
or eastern side. As the front moved north there was the usual
growth of static HQ for 'areas'—initially Naples, Bari, Brindisi
and Taranto. The two armies in Italy were coordinated by HQ
Allied Armies in Italy (AAI), housed in an enormous palace
at Caserta near Naples built in the eighteenth century, which
the successive HQ occupying it had no difficulty in filling. Back
in Algiers there was an even bigger HQ called Allied Forces
(AFHQ) which occupied a great deal of the habitable space in
that city and every hotel. These higher HQ had to deal not only
with operational planning but inter-allied questions and the
government of liberated territories, and had a voracious appetite
for staff and clerical labour. In July, 1944, AFHQ moved to
Caserta and HQ AAI disappeared, but as it became more and
more a sort of civil capital of Italy (to oversimplify) a new HQ
was set up to command operations called Fifteenth Army Group.
BNAF was eventually reduced in scope and wound up as the
logistic base was developed in Italy itself, but the Middle East
command remained a great *place d'armes* and base, units in Italy
being sent there to rest sending reinforcements for the Eighth
Army and the static chain.

The main factors that Lady Maud had to bear in mind were
that there were very few ATS available in Home forces to meet
the bill, that there was no possibility of local recruiting and that
conditions in Italy were harsh. Accommodation was scarce and
primitive even in quite large towns—unlike the Middle East
where there were a great many hutted camps built to house a
transient military population—the country had been ravaged
by war, typhus was raging and the Italian winters are cold, wet
and miserable.

The ATS detachment sent to Eighth Army Rear (administrative)
HQ at Cesena in the winter of 1944–45 had to accept the fact
that it was a mobile HQ and the best that could be expected
was a roof over one's head, sometimes only a tent. The girls
there lived in three cottages without heat, or sanitation, except
for the usual camp arrangements in the garden. Tilly lamps

and a share of the electric light from the HQ generator provided a little light. Each girl had two gallons of water a day for everything; cooking was on hydro-burners in a field kitchen (or on that sooty and dangerous invention called a 'drip-burner', which economically used water and used sump or diesel oil but made the cooks as black as sweeps). Washing was in basins made from cut down oil drums, with a shower in the Mobile Laundry and Bath Unit as a bi-weekly treat. Dame Helen, a great one for the spartan life and for demonstrating that women could put up with severe conditions and discomfort as well as men, would have been delighted.

Africa was a much pleasanter environment but Lady Maud, having weighed up her resources, decided to concentrate on Italy. Ten of a party of twenty newly trained ATS staff officers who came out from England early in 1944 were given appointments in AFHQ in Algiers, but the remainder went on to Naples to fill posts in Signals, 'G(SD)', 'A', 'Q', 'S & T' and Ordnance. (The official records are contradictory here. The returns show ATS deployed until the middle of 1944, but elsewhere it is stated that five ATS staff officers were working in Algiers as early as April, 1943, without mentioning their appointments.) Cutting out BNAF reduced the demand by 3,000, and the ATS force for Italy was made up from a small detachment from Home Forces and larger reinforcements from the Middle East of drafts and whole units. Who arrived first and from where is now somewhat difficult to sort out, but the earliest claim is for a team of clerks, volunteers from Kenya, who joined HQ AAI in Caserta, where their 'house warming' party was attended by General Sir Harold Alexander himself, a kind and typical gesture on his part. About the same time or shortly afterwards came a Polish unit with its British liaison officer, K. Stocker, now a Chief Commander, and later, to be joyously welcomed by their male comrades already deployed in Italy, a contingent of PATS. The ATS had detachments in the field with HQ Eighth Army, as said, and also with HQ Fifth Army's British liaison section, who were looked after by the US Army's WAAC with whom, as Dame Leslie has recorded in her memoirs, a firm and cordial link had been forged.

The ATS and PATS were otherwise deployed around the static chain as clerks, in signal duties, driving ambulances and other transport, and working in hospitals. The first two companies in action were the 600th at Benevento and the 601st at Bari. In May, 1944, the 1st Mediterranean Group with headquarters in Rome was established to look after ATS affairs and Chief Commander K. P. Morrison-Bell was appointed to command from the Middle East. In November the 2nd Group under Senior Commander M. E. Priestley was formed, with a Greek company working the British HQ switchboard there under command.

Some ATS were assigned to teams of the Allied Commission, whose business it was to take over temporarily the administration of newly liberated territory until civil government could be restored. This account of ATS service can appropriately be ended with the saga (here alas, all too baldly recounted) of Junior Commander Goggin in Cremona and Mantua, assisted by a refugee Hungarian doctor whose name is unfortunately not in the record. She succeeded in persuading the US Army to ferry her small unarmed team across the river Po, to be informed by the 34th US Infantry Division that her area had not yet been cleared. Sporadic fighting was still going on between isolated pockets of Germans who, understandably, preferred to surrender to regular British and American troops than trigger-happy bands of Italian partisans, and there was a good deal of sporadic firing. Undeterred the two women set about their work, restarting the machinery for public health, welfare and education, discovering in the course of this that the entire water supply in Mantua was infected and so preventing an epidemic. They also collected the refugees who were wandering about behind the battle-lines and looked after them for two months until the appropriate organization could take them over. There days after Junior Commander Goggin had been in Cremona the German garrison commander emerged from hiding and surrendered to her personally: what a subject for a Shavian dialogue!

If it is still necessary to show what two determined women can achieve, then the work of Junior Commander Goggin and her partner in Italy in 1945 can always be cited as an example.

Across the Atlantic

Five ATS always wearing plain clothes formed part of the clerical staff of the British Military Mission in Washington, until the United States became a belligerent, when everyone went into uniform and the Mission expanded. When the Director (then Chief Controller Knox) visited Washington she was met as usual, with a demand for many more ATS. She decided to discover if there was a field for recruiting in the West Indies, then divided militarily into the North and South Caribbean Areas, and obtained the agreement of the commander of the British Army Staff to the attachment of Controller V. Falkner in December, 1942, with a roving brief covering the West Indies, the United States and Canada to see what should be done.

The Middle East was complicated by the quarrels of politics and religion, the West Indies by something we have come to know only too well—the clash of race and colour, aggravated by different cultural levels in different islands. The West Indians were acutely sensitive to differences in status not only between themselves and the European-born but among themselves as, for instance, between cooks and clerks. Some of the British-born girls were the daughters of rich expatriates and a trifle hoity-toity. They did not at first mix easily with the, by then, far tougher and more professional ATS from Britain, who had no time for such nonsense, and a little time was required for both sides to settle down together. On top of this we are speaking of 1942, it must be remembered, when coloureds were not on the same footing as whites in Washington, and so only whites could be employed there, whereas in the Caribbean it was essential for political reasons for both coloureds and whites to be recruited without discrimination and employed on their merits. These were all problems to be got over by good sense and good management.

The West Indian ATS were occupied in three areas: in the

local garrisons, not easy because the United States Navy had bases in the British West Indies and had snapped up a lot of able girls as civilian staff, in Washington, and a few who volunteered to serve in Britain. By September, 1944, there were fifteen officers and 423 rank and file serving in the United States under Senior Commander P. B. Hammick and this remained the level of manning until the end of the war. By April, 1945, the total strength in the two Caribbean areas was 200, and 100 West Indians volunteered for service in the ATS in Britain.

In their modest way the ATS in America did a great deal of good for Anglo-American relations. The Americans were by no means united in their attitude towards the war. There was a strong anti-war and anti-British feeling in the Middle West, the traditional home of American isolationism, but there were also bonds of affection between the two countries which had survived a good deal of fraying by both sides. The aim, on both sides, was to reduce the first by reasonable argument, and by positive steps to strengthen the second. The Americans themselves, always famous for their kindness and hospitality, made every effort to entertain all ranks, even inviting those who had been ill to convalesce in their homes, and the girls proved good ambassadors. Controller Falkner went on an intensive lecture tour to explain the work of British women at war and was well received everywhere, including Wayne University, Detroit, whose students when last addressed by a British speaker, Lord Halifax, had thrown eggs and tomatoes at him. Their presence in Washington also cemented the link between the ATS and the Canadian Women's Army Corps (CWAC). The two services worked together closely and happily. The Caribbean recruits were trained by the CWAC in Canada, and in 1944 an exchange of officers was begun with thirty ATS attached to the Canadian forces for three months and then thirty Canadians to the Army of Britain.

East Africa

East Africa Command had within its boundaries a source of female staff in the settler community, some of whom were

20   Adventure Training, Malaysia, 1970

21   Women from the six British Services, NATO Women's Conference,
London, 1975

22 *Winter Survival Course Norway, 1975*

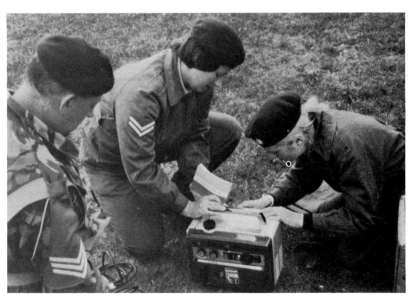

23 *Members of 39 (City of London) Signals Regiment in training*

employed as civilians and some organized as a uniformed voluntary body in the shape of the local independent branch of the FANY. Useful as they were, they could not fully meet the bill for a properly trained military force in either numbers or skills. Accordingly in March, 1943, No. 1 Clerical Company ATS was sent out, followed in November of the same year by No. 2 Company, so that by December the total strength in the command was twelve officers and 474 NCOs and rank and file. In addition a number of NCOs trained in catering duties were brought out to supervise the indigenous cooks and waiters and the Italian prisoner-of-war cooks who staffed the kitchens and messes.

In other theatres, as we have seen, there was always a preliminary reconnaissance by an experienced and senior ATS officer. This was omitted, as the facts of geography and the position of white rank and file in a colonial society were not fully appreciated (it was felt that supervision could be effected by the Deputy Director in Cairo) and there were initial difficulties. There was at first no experienced senior commander to look after the administration and act as the essential link and adviser to the general staff, there was a shortage of administrative staff – one sergeant and one auxiliary for an equivalent battalion strength – and the cost of living was on the high side. The ATS were being given no work or tasks far below their competence. It took about six weeks to become acclimatized. All these minor difficulties were overcome, and the Group settled down to work in what was in many ways a pleasant environment. The Kenya Women's Emergency Organization arranged leave for some of the auxiliaries in private houses and provided a certain amount of social life.

India and the Far East

The ATS effort in India was small, and mainly confined to training the WAC(I), or Women's Auxiliary Corps of India. This had been raised in 1942, but had made little useful progress; Indian society had not yet absorbed the idea of women working outside their traditional occupations and there were the same

9

obstacles to their employment and constraints about accommodation and messing that the WAAC had faced back in 1917. In an attempt to bring the WAC(I) on to a professional footing an ATS team was sent out in July, 1944, under the command of Senior Controller the Countess of Carlisle consisting of administrative officers and instructors together with a woman psychologist and two personnel selection officers with the mission of setting up a selection board, an OCTU and four recruit training centres. This was not an easy task, for Lady Carlisle was to find, just as had been found in Palestine, that politics entered into it (we, with our rigid separation of service loyalties and political affiliations, always seem slightly surprised that this idyllic state of affairs does not obtain in other armies), and in the growing mood for independence it was found that some Indian members of the WAC(I) were prepared to resent foreign tutelage. The effort was made too late to have any effect on the war, which was to be over in a year, but the work of the British team overcame these initial prejudices and broke ground for the formation of the women's service in the future army of independent India and Pakistan.

Apart from this the ATS effort in India was negligible. A few women from the Middle East Command volunteered for service there, but by the time they had arrived the war in Burma was virtually over, the main headquarters (ALFSEA, Allied Land Forces, South-east Asia, and SACSEA, Supreme Allied Headquarters South-East Asia) had moved from India to Kandy in Ceylon. Later SACSEA moved to Singapore. The surrender of Japan obviated the need for a combined operation to liberate Singapore and Malaya, and the work of Lord Louis Mountbatten's command was to clear up the mess and normalize the situation. The ATS were engaged largely in clerical duties, but they had a glimpse of events at a turning point in the history of southern Asia. Corporal Flood, for instance, a stenographer, was at the meeting between Aung San, the Burmese leader and the British representative, General Stopford. The horrors of war were made clear enough from the reports of the death camps in Thailand (typed by batches of ATS) or the sight of repatriated prisoners of war. But southern Asia, and especially the uplands of Ceylon where SACSEA was first located near Kandy, was a far cry from the rigours of AA gun positions in East Anglia, the mud of Italy or the gloomy devastation of Germany. The climate —except during the short monsoon rains—the scenery, and the conditions of service, so briefly enjoyed and, one might add, well deserved, were ideal.

France and the Low Countries

So far we have seen that wherever in the world there were British troops fighting or there were British or Allied headquarters deployed, except in eastern India and Burma, there were ATS working in support of them on the lines of communication or in the bases. The climax of the Allied effort in the west in terms of men and material dwarfed all other British efforts, including the great defensive battles of the Fourteenth Army at Imphal and Kohima and the destruction of the Japanese in Burma, and the part played by the ATS was proportionately greater. The numbers speak for themselves. In South-East Asia and India the total of all ranks deployed was about 250 at the most; the United States, a few more; in East Africa just over 500 at peak strength; in the Middle East, over 5,000 of all nationalities or language groups; Italy 3,000. The ATS strength in north-west Europe in mid-1945 was 9,543. We see the pattern being repeated of the main effort being made in the base—Britain—and the ATS following up as the armies advance and so the ATS story in the grand final act of the war is not of a minor or peripheral effort but a continuation of the huge preparatory effort described in the previous chapter.

The now forgotten deployment of five mixed anti-aircraft regiments Royal Artillery for the defence of Antwerp and Brussels —incidentally the only deployment of women in an operational role in any regular army—belongs to the saga of the ATS part in air defence in the next chapter, while the main account continues after that with the final victory, the occupation of Germany and the course of demobilization, an administrative feat as remarkable in its way and equally fraught with political complications as the original expansion of the force. Here it will be sufficient to note that on 28 July an advanced party of ATS consisting of a small detachment of clerks and two provost corporals arrived with rear headquarters of 21st Army Group in Normandy, still in a tented camp with the girls' bell tents dug in for protection against bombing but luxurious by the standards of northern Italy or the rigours of East Anglia in the 'Diver' belt. There they were joined a month later by the main body. By September the numbers had risen to 781 and to 6,290 by the New Year. This figure includes the strong and many-functioned ATS element in HQ SHAEF (Supreme Headquarters, Allied Expeditionary Force), which included staff officers in the Intelligence Branch (G2), Civil Affairs, Public Relations, Psychological Warfare, Liaison with Allies and personal assistants to the Chief of Staff and his Deputy, as well as six cypher officers, a clerical platoon thirty strong, a mixed motor transport company and several hundred working in the headquarters signal unit. At 21st Army Group there were 120 cooks and mess orderlies, 113 drivers and 220 clerks.

Chapter VIII

Anti-Aircraft Command

W HEN, in 1939, the first eager volunteers for the new Auxiliary Territorial Service stormed the adjutants' office of the Territorial Army some, as recounted, were allotted to the anti-aircraft regiments of the Royal Artillery, where they were given the usual non-combatant jobs. Few then would have believed that they would play an important operational role in a great, prolonged and decisive battle to save the country from defeat in the air. To set this achievement in its proper perspective it is first necessary to describe the structure of the Air Defence of Great Britain (ADGB) and its component, AA Command.

The Royal Air Force was responsible for our air defence, and its two weapons, its sword and shield, as it were, were Fighter Command and AA Command. AA Command was an army composed entirely of guns and searchlights deployed throughout the country, moved about as necessary. It was organized, like an army, into divisions and brigades. (Later the divisions were called groups but we need not be concerned with such detail here.) Brigades consisted of varying numbers of regiments, usually of three batteries of two troops of four guns each. Operationally the brigades and regiments were allotted to 'gun defended areas' — cities, ports, factories or other vital points — which were tied through 'gun operation rooms' to the nearest Fighter Group HQ, it being the business of the RAF to orchestrate the various means of defence. The role of AA Command was to raise the regiments, train them, administer them, think out new means of hitting the raiding aircraft and in short to create the weapon as well as to use it as directed by ADGB. By 1940 it already had a strong ATS support element — clerks, cooks, telephonists, orderlies, waitresses and so on — and an ATS chain of command ran down through the structure. In fact there was nothing different in principle from the other organizations described so far.

As early as 1938, however, it had occurred to more than one Territorial adjutant to see if the women could do something better. In one case, certainly, the ATS volunteers were allowed to try their hand on the fire-control instruments; it was difficult to keep their interest if all they could do on 'drill nights' was to practice marching and saluting while the men worked on the guns. There may have been other unofficial experiments along these lines, but the first official one was by the newly appointed commander of the 1st AA Division. Major-General Pile, as he then was, was a forward-thinking, radically-minded officer who had exchanged out of the Royal Artillery in 1923 into the Royal Tank Regiment as he believed it to be a revolutionary arm and the herald of the warfare of the future, but had been summoned back to the guns to assist in the belated expansion of our air defences. General Pile was a man ideally fitted to wage a unique and prolonged war governed more by science and technology than by conventional tactics, and one continually demanding new ideas and fresh initiatives. He was to lead AA Command with distinction from 1939 to 1945. In 1938 he had invited Miss Caroline Haslett, an engineer of note, to visit his batteries at practice and advise him if any of the work could be done by women. She considered that they could do all of it, except the heavy work on the guns, such as hefting ammunition or manhandling them into and out of action.

His foresight was rewarded in 1940, when he was faced simultaneously with the need to expand the Command and a shortage of 19,000 officers and men. Inevitably in any inter-arm tussle for manpower AA Command, a purely defensive organization, was likely to come off the worst, and this proved to be the case; it was to be raided continually for manpower for the field army until the end of the war. Pile demanded to be allowed to use women operationally on the gun-sites. This of course ran into an immediate political difficulty, as the public were averse to women being deliberately exposed to danger from enemy action, and violently opposed to them operating weapons in any circumstances. (The moral objections to mixing with soldiers and adjacent billeting hung over the ATS like a cloud, but this extended over the whole field of their activities.) Sir James Grigg, Under-Secretary of State for War, declared the proposal as 'breath-taking and revolutionary', but in the end there was no escaping it: a successful air defence was an even stronger political imperative than the possible moral and physical dangers to the daughters of the nation. Winston Churchill was more positive. He said that any general who saved him 40,000 men of fighting age had gained the equivalent of a victory. Pile, and the ATS, did rather better than that: 56,000 women were employed in the Command by September, 1943. Churchill proved a stout supporter of both the ATS and AA Command. He found himself in tune with the innovating Pile, and frequently consulted him, sometimes on strategic subjects quite outside air defence. His daughter Mary joined the ATS and served as a junior commander in one of the mixed batteries.

Early in 1941 it was agreed to form fully integrated batteries, with the women operating the fire-control instruments and the men the guns, and by August of the same year an experimental mixed battery was deployed, partly as a public relations exercise, in Richmond Park, not far from the headquarters of AA Command.

The women were joining an army as unique in its outlook and *esprit de corps* as the Eighth Army or the Fourteenth Army. AA Command was somewhat self-conscious of its home-based passive role, bearing public abuse philosophically when it failed to shoot down every raider in sight with its inadequate equipment, or remaining silent for reasons it could not make public. It was highly technical and proud of it. Except for its regular Royal Artillery senior officers, it was almost entirely a Territorial and citizen army. Its war was dull and trying, the endless vigil on bleak and isolated gun-sites being rewarded at long intervals with brief moments of action. For these it had to remain continuously at the concert pitch of training, and then display great accuracy and the strictest fire discipline. AA artillery shared none of the glamour of Fighter Command RAF, and until the 'V-1' pilotless aircraft appeared, was seldom rewarded with the credit for a hit. Its discipline and its morale were, therefore, of a special kind, as also had to be the leadership given to its men and women.

The ATS were only employed operationally in the heavy branch, with the 3·7 inch, 4·5 inch and 5·25 inch guns which fired to high altitudes and were used in conjunction with an elaborate fire control set-up. Already air defence was 'sophisticated', and as the war went on it became more so, but in simple terms the problem was to identify a hostile aircraft, track it, measure its height (range) and bearing, which were continually changing, and feed the results into a computer which passed the necessary data to the guns. Even at the speed of those days while the salvo of shells travelled to the point of lay—some 20 seconds—the target might have moved two miles or more. The system had to arrange a fatal rendezvous in space, so to speak.

Later in the war there were gun-laying radars, proximity fuses, better predictors and fully automated laying of guns, but the basic system which most veterans will recall was for a spotter to pick up the target, a detachment operating an optical heightfinder to produce ranges, a delicate operation involving the adjustment of the image of the moving target in the field of view of what was in effect a large double-vision telescope and which automatically displayed the range on a scale, and a tracker to follow it for bearing. Another detachment operated the 'predictor' which 'predicted' where the target would be by the time the guns were ready to fire; it was an early type of computer, from which electrical impulses were passed along cables to the guns close by, where the layers, ignoring the actual targets, followed a display on dials in front of them. The shell, or shells, were not expected to hit the target. The lethal effect was obtained by bursting them in the air close to it and filling the target area with a cloud of steel splinters ('shrapnel', as it was commonly and incorrectly termed). Only the fuse-length had to be passed vocally to the guns. At first it was feared that women's voices would not carry, but this was countered by the old exercise of putting them in pairs on training to call out orders and repeat them back across the breadth of a parade ground.

A New Zealander who joined a battery at Droitwich recounted to the author that when she went home for her first leave she asked her family at tea-time the somewhat unusual question, would they like to hear her shout? The result astonished them.

This procedure although endlessly practised, was difficult enough to execute with speed and precision by daylight in peace against a slow-moving drogue or a drone appearing from an expected direction: it was a very different matter after tumbling out at night to take post amid the crash of falling bombs and the roar of gun-fire. It was a test that the ATS passed repeatedly with flying colours; nor did they fail to meet the whole challenge of the anti-aircraft service. Danger there was, although it is fair to say that in many ways a gun-site was safer than a street of terraced houses in a manufacturing town. It is good to record that very few women were killed or wounded, but when they were their comrades stepped into their place unmoved, for the moment, and without hesitation. Their true achievement was that their morale and efficiency never sagged.

The formation of fully integrated mixed batteries posed problems not only of administration but of mental adjustment by both sexes, and it was wisely decided to make this as easy as possible by forming at first whole new regiments instead of posting women into existing batteries where the newcomers might be resented as interlopers.

The ATS structure aimed at was an AA brigade HQ where the brigadier was advised by a Deputy Director ATS (a chief commander, or lieutenant-colonel). In each mixed regiment the ATS were grouped together for the purpose of administration, records and discipline into a company commanded by a senior commander (major) at RHQ, with a junior commander and two subalterns in each battery, which gave a subaltern to each troop. It will be understood that the ATS continued to provide substantial administrative support as well as forming part of the 'firing battery', to use the expressive old Gunner term.

The first mixed battery, the pilot model, was deployed in Richmond Park, where it excited great interest. Who was first in the field is difficult to deduce accurately from the records, but it seems the first mixed regiment to be formed was the 129th, the first to fire in action from a war gun-site was the 132nd, on 21 November, 1941, and the first 'kill', in April, 1942, by 451 Battery, 133rd Regiment. What is perfectly clear, and of more consequence, is the method of raising the new regiments. The authority, based on experience, was the pamphlet on the *Formation, Training and Command of Mixed Heavy Anti-Aircraft Batteries, Royal Artillery* (notified in Army Council Instructions, 29 April, 1942.) This was clear, concise and to the point. The aims of training were fourfold: operational fitness; administrative efficiency; correct military relationships between ATS and RA (the same standards to be applied to both sexes, no favouritism, punctilious saluting, the senior officer or NCO present, male or female, to be in command and his or her orders obeyed by all); and the importance of off-duty occupations, games, recreation and education; with a note to the effect that all four were equally important and none were to be neglected in favour of concentration on gunnery. The ATS officers were responsible for ATS discipline, and the battery commander 'should from the start insist on the rigid application of this rule'. ATS should take their share of all duties within their physical capacity, but would only provide an unarmed picquet by day, the men being responsible for armed guards after dark. This was waived in 93rd Searchlight Regiment where the ATS provided their own sentries armed with pick-helves. The original charter made it clear that women would only man fire-control instruments and never the guns, and that ATS officers would be given just enough gunnery instruction to understand the nature of the task, but never be operationally employed. In action, or training for action, the 'Royal Artillery Gun Position Officer and his male subordinates would take complete command of the Troop'.

So much for the official skeleton. Fortunately the first battery commander of 481st (M) HAA Battery published a delightful account of its formation in the Journal of the Royal Artillery Institution which breathes flesh on to these dry bones. The method employed was to assemble the new battery complete at a special mixed HAA training regiment in three groups: a small cadre consisting of the officers, the Battery-Sergeant Major, the Battery Quartermaster-Sergeant, and twenty odd bombardiers and gunners; a squad of ATS recruits from an ATS Training Centre, kitted up and having completed their basic military training, and another of gunner recruits from a Training Regiment RA in a similar state. The cadre was given a brisk refresher course in AA gunnery and tactics while the men and women were first trained on their respective equipments and then welded together in teams. The rank and file were very young and excitable and at first the female detachments chattered incessantly in a most unmilitary manner, but once this phase was overcome progress was rapid. The verdict was that compared to men ATS were inferior as spotters (possibly because male juvenile interest was attracted by the mechanical details of aircraft and the female was not), predictor work was about equal and heightfinding superior. Discipline was good and, as elsewhere, the gloomy prophecies about ATS morals which seemed to give some Jeremiahs actual pleasure were confounded. The patent anomalies of having two disciplinary codes and two chains of command became workable once the full understanding and mutual regard that should exist in every good regiment was established between the RA and ATS officers. As for sexual relationships it was not the illicit which proved a nuisance but marriage! The regulations insisted that married couples might not serve together, a heart-ache eased as far as possible by cross-postings to different batteries in the same regiment.

The battery commander's personal reactions to this novel task were not untypical. He himself was a regular and a field gunner to his roots, sadly disappointed at being relegated through illness from a field regiment about to go overseas, but he ended a fervent believer in the mixed principle and developed a strong affection and respect for the ATS. 'My men and girls are great', he wrote, and he speaks of the 'sea of young and eager faces' he saw before him when he first addressed them, and records with pride that when the training period was over the whole battery was sent on block leave with orders to rendezvous at a railway station where a special train was to take them to their war-site on 18 December, a week before Christmas, and that there was only *one* absentee—and *he* was down with scarlet fever. Deservedly this officer went on to command a regiment. He also played a considerable part in drafting the official pamphlet.

No attempt was made to make the two sexes mix. Confounding the Grundy's, the girls (for most of them were) at first completely segregated themselves off duty, and the men were equally stand-offish. Only later did they come together, and then the firmest of bonds developed. Dame Frances Coulshed recalls that when, in Europe, the women of a battery were moved by air for administrative convenience while the men took the equipment by road convoy to their new war-site and went on to the airfield with transport to collect their ATS, from their behaviour 'you'd have thought they hadn't seen each other for years!'

It is pleasant to record that femininity was not wholly suppressed. Loud squeals, 'Ahs' and 'Oohs' greeted the first acclimatization rounds from the admittedly noisy 3·7 inch HAA gun, and one Divisional Commander was much amused by the reaction of some instrument numbers at the end of a very successful 'series' (practice shoot) which culminated in actually hitting the target sleeve: 'They danced about hugging each other and crowing with delight'. But in case this might give the wrong impression it should be emphasized that in mixed batteries, as in every kind of good fighting unit, drill, training, duties in action, even moving about the gun site, parading for routine chores and so on were all carried out with the utmost smartness and military precision. The photographs of the ATS muffled up in layers of winter clothing do little justice to their personal turnout and well-ironed spotless uniform, blanco'd stripes and lanyards and dazzling toe-caps. Every surface on their equipment was painted or polished.

The net result was the addition to the order of battle of AA Command of seventy highly serviceable heavy regiments,* but it

---

* This is an approximate figure. The total number of heavy AA regiments in Home Forces at one time or another was 101, but during the process of expansion some were posted overseas and later, as General

must be added that the process was not completed entirely without friction. There were two issues which had to be fought out—the actual status of the ATS, and how far they, and the officers in particular, should be allowed to play an operational part. There were clashes of opinion at the highest level. The Gunners, and General Pile himself favoured this view, would have preferred to have absorbed the women completely into the Royal Artillery, although this was quite contrary to the ATS charter and a policy already settled. Understandably they tenaciously held a view not always obvious to those unfamilier with the age-old British 'regimental' system which used to foster the *esprit de corps* and without which a good morale and efficiency cannot exist. Neither a battery nor any other combat unit can be run in the same way as a pay office or a petrol depot. Moreover it was not long before the ATS in the firing batteries, for the most natural of reasons, began to identify with the Royal Artillery: 'We all wanted to be Gunners', recalls Dame Frances Coulshed. When Chief Controller Knox learnt of this trend she came down on it like a ton of bricks. Addressing one battery she reminded the women that they were ATS first and foremost and could be posted anywhere, which upset them. Her point of view was understandable, for as a general rule for the full value of the ATS to be realized there had to be flexibility of posting. It was more than a storm in a tea-cup, as an important principle of personnel management was involved, but the apparent contradiction of duel loyalty can always be bridged by common-sense and good will. The Gunners were regularly faced with it themselves as between their own chain of command so jealously preserved and their tradition of support to 'their' infantry or tanks, equally insisted upon. As for the rationale for the ATS chain of command the letter already quoted on page 87 which put it so clearly was in fact written to Lieutenant-Colonel Naylor, whose account of building up a mixed battery has just

---

Pile states in his despatches, he was ordered to reduce by no fewer than 100 mixed batteries, or 33 equivalent regiments. After the success of the mixed idea some existing male regiments were converted, so that the total strength in terms of units was always changing.

been mentioned. ATS control of discipline and ATS administration therefore remained unmodified, but as integration progressed and understanding improved it ceased to be an irritant; on the contrary, its real advantages were perceived.

At the same time some sensible concessions were made to regimental feeling, without impugning the loyalty owed to the Service. The ATS in regiments of Royal Artillery were allowed to wear the grenade badge on their blouses and the AA Command formation sign on their sleeves, and the white Gunner lanyard instead of the ATS one. Sergeants put up the gun-badge above their chevrons, like sergeants RA, and on site – and on site only – corporals were addressed as 'bombardier' and auxiliaries (privates) as 'Gunner'. (The paragraph in the official pamphlet authorizing this was due to the personal intervention of the Prime Minister, who took a paternal interest in 481 Battery deployed in Hyde Park.) The feelings of the ATS in the batteries on the question of their affiliation to the Royal Artillery within these constraints remained deep and strong.

The question of operational duties was even more vexed. It was a sophistry to pretend that a boundary could be drawn somewhere between a plotting room or a command post, operating a predictor or physically pulling the firing lever of a gun. The situation became more absurd when the advance of automation was such that the guns were fired by remote control when on target, from the command post. Women who could operate a predictor or a GL set were perfectly capable of following the range and bearing dials on the gun itself a few yards off, and women were capable of adjusting an automatic fuse-setter or even of taking over a light 40 mm AA gun complete. The moral objections – to taking life – were less tenable when the target was a pilotless V-1. Stories persist that in the early days, before the mixed batteries were ever formed, women helped out in the gun detachments in sites on Merseyside. However, and wisely, the division of role was enforced as long as AA Command existed. It was fixed for convenience and as a concession to popular prejudice at any job inside the gun detachment.

When the ATS took over operation of the searchlights the authorities were faced with a dilemma. Each light was provided with a tripod-mounted light machine gun to deter any raider who attempted to dive down the beam and attack it, but only a male was allowed to man it (who also proved useful to hand-start the heavy diesel generator providing the power for the light), but what would be the consequences if it was known that with each of these isolated parties of women was billeted a single male soldier? Such were the moral and ethical problems which continued to bedevil the ATS as they strove to get on with the war!

The ban on officer participation in the War Office pamphlet is more difficult to explain, unless it was due to insistence inside the ATS Directorate that their officers should stick to their proper work of the discipline and well-being of the women. It was gradually relaxed. This was hardly enough to keep them fully occupied, even if given a share of the routine chores which would otherwise entirely fall on the male officers, such as 'Q', messing and education. It was also a waste of talent, for a proportion of officers were educated up to degree standard. More important, it is a *sine qua non* of leadership that an officer should be capable of any of the ordinary skills of his men and it was galling for ATS officers to be left out and so lose 'face' in front of their subordinates. As one put it, their role could degenerate into that of a 'nanny' in a nursery of grown-up children. As a result in spite of regulations or instructions to the contrary the ATS officers began to infiltrate the 'firing battery' area. At 481 Battery's debut at live practice before occupying its war-sites Junior Subaltern Diana Hewett, aged twenty, took her troop through a perfect 'series' in front of the admiring Instructors-in-Gunnery (a much feared and devastatingly critical body of men). Later she was sent on a radar course and came out top—an achievement to be outshone by her colleague Isobel Murdoch, who became a radar instructor. Diana Hewett was also possibly one of the first to act as 'tactical control officer', at an exercise watched by the divisional commander, so the practice was certainly condoned, and there is evidence to show that it spread widely, but how far exactly is now difficult to state with any historical exactitude. (Certainly the assertions in the article in the *Journal of the Artillery Institution* were never contradicted.) Mrs Fraser-Tytler, General Pile's senior ATS adviser for most of the war and completely in his confidence, states that she firmly turned a blind eye on it.

The Royal Artillery provided two other areas for ATS employment. Throughout the war searchlights were an essential part of ADGB for assisting both the RAF fighters and the Gunners. Crude at first, they were later 'married' to the 'Elsie' radar and with radar, light, generator and radio link to HQ, each site required technical expertise to run effectively. In 1941, unpromising though it at first seemed, some ATS were formed into an experimental searchlight troop; unpromising, because the sites, not like those of guns in a complete troop, were of single lights distributed in a certain pattern over the countyside, and on the face of it daunting for small isolated parties of women without weapons or nearby assistance and largely unaccustomed to the loneliness and darkness of wet fields and woods, full of strange noises from the English countryside in winter. Women were carefully selected for intelligence and physique, trained in operating and maintaining their equipment, and given a 'fitness for role' test. This involved finding the route to their site, given only the six-figure map reference, driving their vehicles to it, and emplacing their light and generator, having removed the ones they found occupying it, which involved some strenuous winching and towing under the critical eyes of the instructors.

Gradually ATS troops were added to the existing male regiments and carefully observed to see how the women made out in these unfamiliar conditions, and when they had been proved they were all grouped together on 25 November, 1942, into an expanded, all-female unit—the 93rd Searchlight Regiment RA—1,500 strong with a Royal Artillery commanding officer and an ATS adjutant. Radio maintenance was carried out by an all-ATS team under Subaltern Swennel and twenty-four telemechanics attached to the regiment. General Pile has paid the 93rd Regiment a generous tribute in his autobiography for their military efficiency, the way they turned their huts and sites into little homes, with gardens and pets, and their devotion to duty. HRH The Princess Royal visited the Regiment on 21 March, 1943, soon after it was deployed, in Essex.

The other ATS contribution was to the rocket batteries. To make up for the serious deficiencies in light AA guns a crude, cheap free-flight rocket and launcher had been produced with a fuse to burst it at the correct height. Sixty-four launchers were grouped together, and the idea was to point them in the general direction of an attacking aircraft with the aid of a GL radar in the hope that if one of this huge salvo did not connect with it at least the pilot might be put off his stroke. When, in 1942, there was yet another demand on AA Command for fit men for the field army the rocket groups changed over to a system of mixed manning, each with a controlling cadre of Royal Artillery, a pool of 4,000 Home Guard working on a shift basis round the clock, and four officers and 170 NCOs and rank and file of the ATS.

In a condensed narrative like this many amusing anecdotes are perforce omitted, but two are worth recounting. When 481 Battery was deployed in Hyde Park (many will remember seeing it there, bulled to the nines with gleaming steel and brass work and immaculate paint) and Mary Churchill was the ATS junior commander, a message from the Prime Minister's office to the battery commander asked if he may look in and visit it en route from the Commons to Downing Street, which gave much pleasure. It was after dark, and the unbriefed male sentry on guard, his wits momentarily paralysed by the august apparition revealed by the dim light inside the large car demanded its identity card, which was produced after some terrifying rumbles. Then: 'You did quite right, my boy'.

In Aberdeen, after a severe raid which caused casualties in the city the men and women of the 128th Regiment found themselves suddenly boycotted. People turned aside, shops refused to serve them and they were even insulted. Enquiries revealed that it was because they were being blamed for the casualties. This was unfair, because the 'gun defended area' was the harbour, which was completely undamaged. The Royal Artillery commander decided to call in the aid of the Lord Provost, and it was arranged to take a party of three coachloads of businessmen, shopkeepers, journalists and other influential persons to visit the batteries and see them at work. By the greatest of good fortune this demonstration was abruptly cancelled in favour of action with live ammunition as the arrival of the visitors coincided with a four-plane raid in full view and broad daylight. The good burgesses of Aberdeen, when not forced to take cover, had a close view of the regiment at work, which led not only to a resumption of cordial relations but eulogies for the 'gun-girls'.

Of deeds of valour there are few to record; the air defence battle did not offer much opportunity, but of examples of steadiness in action and presence of mind there are many. The first woman to be killed in action was Private J. Caveney of the 148th Regiment, by a bomb splinter when at the predictor. The casualty drill was imperturbably followed and the spotter, G. Keel, stepped in so promptly that firing was not interrupted. Privates Clements and Dunsmore were both injured when 'taking post' by being blown over by a stick of bombs dropped across the troop position; after the engagement was over it was found that Clements had injured her knee and Dunsmore had been working with a dislocated shoulder. Private M. M. Johnson, an ambulance driver, burned herself badly when she made a brave attempt to drag a survivor from an RAF aircraft she saw crash as she was driving by. Private M. J. Morris, another driver, repeatedly drove her vehicle into the blazing inferno of an ammunition dump, ferrying in men and fire-fighting equipment. Corporal A. E. Brown, cook on a site hit by a V-1 weapon which killed one woman and wounded two others, produced the mid-day meal from her damaged cook-house exactly on time! Sergeant M. A. McVey showed the greatest presence of mind when a succession of V-1s landed on the RAF station at Biggin Hill, wrecking the ATS quarters. She had only left the rescue operations there to return to her post in the Gun Operations Room to find that it too had been hit, and set about bringing reliefs for the injured and putting it into working order again.

Such feats would not be beyond the call of duty for men and should not be regarded as such for women, but they deserve mention.

By 1944 the Luftwaffe had ceased to be a serious strategic threat. 'The preparations for D-Day were completed and the invasion launched, covered by a great concentration of ADGB and field army AA artillery without any interference, but British intelligence had for some time been aware that the Germans had in preparation what were to become known as 'Vengeance Weapons' 1 and 2. The V-1, variously known as the 'doodlebug', the 'buzz-bomb' or the 'diver', was what is now termed a 'cruise-missile'—a small, very fast pilotless aircraft fitted with a large high-explosive warhead and a crude form of guidance which was supposed to make it fly a straight and level course and then dive on to its target. It had a fair chance of hitting a small town, but was erratic in its performance. While it could never have altered the course of the war, unchecked it would have caused heavy casualties, and had adverse results on public morale, still doggedly holding up, but stretched by the long years of the blitz. The 'V' bombardment began on 16 June. The victory over the V-1s scored by the RAF and AA Command in its 'Operation Diver' was a triumphant culmination of ADGB's war, and of the greatest technical interest, but it falls outside the scope of this book. It is sufficient to say that it fell into three phases, the first the establishment of a defensive belt along the south coast which ended when the Allied armies cleared the Channel coast of France, the second when the east coast from Clacton to Yarmouth became an indiscriminate target and the third in the autumn and winter when the V-1s were used locally against the base installations of 21st Army Group in Belgium. The ATS played a full part, needless to say, in a battle in which the official figures tell enough of the story for our purpose. After a slow start, as new tactics, new gunnery methods and new equipment were brought into play, the numbers of missiles hit out of the total routed through the defensive belt of guns of all kinds rose from a meagre 17 per cent to 74 per cent and in one glorious week 82 per cent was recorded. It was summer, and a note of exhilaration can be detected in the recollections of the period at not only success, but visible success.

The East Anglian battle was more dour. It was winter, and the low coast line put the spotters at a disadvantage, so observation towers were built on the sites, from which exposed position the instrument numbers were free to speculate what their chances were if the approaching missile was hit without being exploded and landed in their site, which was a continuing hazard of anti-V-1 engagements, as the first mixed battery to shoot one down nearly learnt to its cost. As it burst into flames the women, deaf to the order to get under cover, stood cheering as it shot overhead and blew in the troop command post, fortunately without hurting anyone.

The total ATS battle casualties over the whole war were very low (389 killed and wounded) but Operation Diver was the costliest period. The figures for the quarter ending September, 1944, are one officer killed and three wounded, ten rank and file killed and one died of wounds and 128 wounded; in no other quarter did they exceed double figures and only once over forty.

The third area of deployment was Belgium. Antwerp was a port vital to the war effort, and the V-1 effort was turned on to that city. Between 12 October, 1944, and 15 March, 1945, 5,960 V-1s struck the city, killing 731 soldiers and 3,515 civilians. A new 'Diver' belt had to be deployed to protect it and also Brussels. The V-1s were an awkward target, being very fast, with speeds up to 400 m.p.h. and flying in a height band which was at the bottom of the HAA gun range and the top of the light AA. Only the ADGB regiments with full automation and the new predictors and radars had mastered the technique. Accordingly the 21st Army Group's own guns were deployed forward towards the Rhine and in November, 1944, five mixed regiments were brought out from England. Senior Commander Coulshed (later Brigadier Dame Frances Coulshed and a future Director, WRAC) was appointed Deputy Assistant Director ATS at GHQ Anti-Aircraft Troops. Their score was nineteen V-1s.

The winter of 1944 was very cold and conditions on site severe.

There was little coal for heating, even the inside of the Nissen huts were decorated with icicles and there was a great deal of sawing of firewood. Frost is tolerable, but the mud of the thaw was Russian in its depth. The tracks collapsed, and essential supplies were passed by human chain from the nearest ground hard enough to bear a vehicle. The girls were by then, however, robust enough to stand any amount of hard work and active service conditions. It had already been noticed that once the ATS ration scale had been increased to the same size as the mens', what with fresh air, hard work, games and physical training they had all outgrown their first issue of uniform. During Operation Diver, when there was a certain amount of public fuss about their living in tents, their health was excellent and sick parades dwindled to almost nothing, and this continued throughout the tour in Belgium.

There the ATS might have thought themselves safe from their well-wishers, but a hare was started from an unexpected quarter. There were regular visits to Brussels, arranged by the admirable Princesse de Ligne's Welfare Organization, allowing 48 hours in the only gay capital in Europe with beds with sheets and hot baths. There one young lady described to her new friend, in the United States Navy, the rigours of service in the ATS on a gun site (naturally something strange to a sailor, especially a sailor on dry land on the Lines of Communication) and he was so horrified that he wrote to the Queen with a copy to the Prime Minister. AA Command had had four years experience of this sort of thing, but it seriously upset the staff at HQ AA Troops. Fortunately their DADATS was able to reassure them and the typhoon in the teacup subsided.

This brings us almost but not quite to the end of the story. Immediately hostilities ended Frances Coushed saw that with the threat removed there was nothing to hold an air defence unit together, and for those ATS who were not due shortly for demobilization she arranged conversion courses to train them as ordnance storewomen or clerks, whose standards proved so high that there were demands for as many more as possible from the headquarters of the Army of Occupation in Germany.

After the war was over AA Command continued in being for some time. Some very advanced gun weapon-systems were under research, and as the Territorial Army was reconstituted mixed regiments of anti-aircraft artillery reappeared in its order of battle. In 1949 when the Women's Royal Army Corps was raised as a regular part of the army there was at first no opportunity for them to serve overseas with a field force AA unit, but in 1952 a mixed battery was added to the Gibralter defence. In 1954 the Princess Royal, as assiduous as ever in her duties as Controller Commandant, visited the battery, and named the WRAC accommodation 'The Princess Royal's Block'. It was not to last. In 1955 it was decided as a matter of policy to dismantle AA Command completely, and the mixed batteries disappeared. On 18 October, 1955, General Sir Frederick Pile, representing the Royal Regiment of Artillery, presented to the Director of the Corps (Brigadier, now Dame, Mary Railton) a silver model of the typical equipment of AA Command, the Ordnance QF 3·7 inch heavy anti-aircraft gun, which now rests in the Corps Museum at Guildford. Veterans of AA Command were on parade to watch the presentation, and marched off to the music of the band of the Royal Artillery. So, with deep regret on both sides, the close ties which had bound the Royal Artillery and the ATS and the Women's Royal Army Corps together were severed.

Chapter IX

The Corps Today

WHEN the war was ended the armed forces were immediately plunged into what can be described as organized chaos. For economic, political and human reasons it was essential to dismantle the huge British war machine; one, it must be remembered, which embraced the national resources more completely than in any other country, as the total commitment of all able-bodied women without dependents had shown. At the same time an economical and efficient peace establishment had to be designed and constructed. It was a painful and difficult process, and many famous corps and regiments were to feel the keen edge of the axe and even be cut down.

One of the casualties of peace might easily have been the women's services, who at best could have hoped for relegation to reserve or Territorial Army status. It is a measure, therefore of the nation's appreciation that it was decided to retain them as a voluntary, regular component of the armed forces. The first public statement to this effect was made in May, 1946, to be followed by another by the Secretary of State for War in November, who spoke for all three services and gave details of the interim plan. As it would take some time to pass the necessary legislation, women would continue to be recruited on an emergency engagement on the wartime pattern, and at the same time serving, or recently demobilized women of all ranks were invited to make 'extended service engagements' to serve for varying numbers of years (three, four or five for officers and two, three or four for servicewomen) and so keep the services in being while the plans were being hammered out.

As regards the ATS and the War Office the atmosphere had completely changed since the demobilization of 1918–21 and the negative period between the wars. The decision to retain the ATS and convert it into a regular Corps, with a corresponding Territoral Army component was, to quote Dame Leslie Whateley's own words, 'A foregone conclusion and there was no dissent on the part of the authorities concerned'. The service had the powerful support of General Sir Ronald Adam, the great war-time Adjutant-General, who asked Dame Leslie to stay on as Director until the middle of 1946 to undertake the ground-work.

This historic decision may have been arrived at smoothly enough, but the task of realizing it, which fell to the next Director, Dame Mary Tyrwhitt, proved long, troublesome and frustrating and involved a great deal of hard bargaining before the nesessary Bill could be drafted and passed through Parliament to become law. This, by our peacetime system, was inevitable from the moment public expenditure was involved and, in addition, the three services each had their highly individual outlook, problems and aspirations which had to be reconciled to ensure some degree of parity in terms of rank, status, pay and terms of service. (To make matters more difficult the legislation for the future WRAC and WRAF could be combined in a single Bill, but the Navy elected to act independently.)

While all this was being thrashed out the ATS led an uneasy and uncertain existence. The speed and size of the demobilization machine was difficult to control, one reason being that the very staffs responsible were disappearing on demobilization and being replaced at a speed calculated to cause confusion. Some women, uninformed about the progress of the planning and the terms, may have been ejected willy-nilly. Colonel Lucy Davies, the present Deputy Controller Commandant, recalls that when she was sent her 'demob' papers she was serving overseas. Acting on advice, she served on without any official existence until the Corps was more organized.

Eventually the preliminaries were complete and on 5 February, 1948, the Secretary of State, by then Mr Emmanuel Shinwell, was able to make a formal submission to the Crown for permission to raise a corps of women for the Regular Army and the Territorial

Army. The proposed title had to contain the words 'women's,' 'army' and 'corps,' as containing the essential minimum of information, and the Army Council further recommended that the distinction 'Royal' should be bestowed in recognition of the services rendered by the ATS, and that Her Majesty the Queen should be appointed the Commandant-in-Chief. This received the Royal approval, but it took months more for the bill to become law and the Women's Royal Army Corps finally came into existence on 1 February, 1949.

The role and structure of the new Corps was broadly based on the experience of the ATS in the war. Its charter was succinct and elastic: 'to provide replacements for officers and men in such employment as may be specified by the Army Council from time to time.' It was to continue to be a non-combatant corps, barred from carrying arms, acting in support of the arms and services and subject, with certain safeguards, to military law. Its administration, discipline and well-being was primarily the responsibility of the officers of the Corps, however the service women were deployed, and representatives of the Director, as before, were positioned appropriately in the command chain.

Compared with the war years the employments offered initially were few: clerks, drivers, switchboard operators, cooks, storewomen and a few AA instrument numbers. This modest beginning was probably for the best, because there were many tough administrative problems to be solved and many more administrative battles to be fought. One of the toughest problems concerned the selection of officers for regular commissions. The hard school of war experience had produced an echelon of able officers who at first were all eager to join, but there was a limit to their patience, and as first the months and then the years went by without any firm prospects they left in a steady stream to seek careers elsewhere. Among those who remained and who had satisfactorily filled vacancies in the war years there were many who were to fail the rigorous peacetime selection procedures which every officer, male or female, now seeking a regular career had to face. This was a great grief to many loyal hearts and a source of anguish all round.

The new regular army had to be run with the utmost economy—when has it not?—and by the rules of the game every departmental head has to fight for his share of the vote. Quartering and accommodation were a great problem, for although the wartime women stoically endured rugged conditions, when it came to recruiting very young women (at eighteen, or seventeen and a half with parental consent) squalid conditions based on wartime hutted camps built for another purpose were hardly likely to attract them or win over their parents. Dame Mary Railton, who was Director from 1954 to 1967, recalls that there was always a fight for something or another going on (a state of affairs by no means peculiar to the Corps), but administrative battles, so engrossing at the time are soon forgotten and if not their details are too tedious to recount. Nevertheless the important progress made by the Corps under her Directorship, notably in the introduction of promotion examinations and educational qualifications for promotion to warrant and non-commissioned rank must be mentioned. Dame Mary Railton became the first Deputy Controller Commandant. The unobtrusive but immensely valuable part in this process played by the late Controller Commandant, the Princess Royal has been gratefully acknowledged by all the Directors during this period. Every Director recalls her understanding of the outlook of the Corps, of the problems facing it and her support and advice. Her loss was keenly felt, and it was therefore a source of great satisfaction when Her Royal Highness the Duchess of Kent was gazetted Controller-Commandant in her place on 28 February, 1967. This happily, was the Golden Jubilee year of all three of the women's services in the armed forces, and was appropriately celebrated. Dame Regina Evans, then chairman of the Women's Royal Army Corps Association, played an important part in organizing the various functions and ceremonies.

Throughout this period the Corps was steadily establishing its reputation at home and overseas as a valuable part of the army; not yet a 'peacetime' army but very much a 'peace-keeping' army, involved in active operation which have barely ceased since 1945. The Corps shared their drudgery and when necessary their dangers, then in Cyprus as now in Ireland, where over 200 servicewomen are working at present. Gradually its responsibilities grew. It is sufficient to let the facts speak for themselves. Today, with a regular strength of some 320 officers and 4,000 servicewomen and 150 and 2,000 in the TAVR, thirty-five employments are open, a variety of skills impossible to précis with justice:

Administrative Assistant
Analyst (Special Intelligence)
Artificer (Instrument)
Artificer (Telecommunications)
Bandswoman
Combat Radioman
Clerk
Clerk (Assistant Programmer)
Clerk (Royal Army Pay Corps)
Clerk (Shorthand Writer)
Communication Centre Operator
Cooks (Two groups)
Data Telegraphist
Driver
Experimental Assistant (Gunnery)
Hairdresser
Kennelmaid
Medical Orderly
Mess Caterer
Mess Steward
Movement Operator
Military Policewoman – Provost
Military Policewoman (Special Investigation Branch)
Operator (Electronic Warfare)
Operator Intelligence and Security
Postal and Courier Operator
Physical Training Instructor
Radio Telegraphist
Radar Operator (Light Air Defence)
Rider/Groom
Stewardess
Storewoman (Royal Army Ordnance Corps)
Switchboard Operator
Technical Clerk

The primary task of the officers is, as in all regiments, the care of the rank and file, but in addition, as in all other corps or regiments, specialist jobs which include motor transport, catering, communications – the bond between the Corps and the Royal Corps of Signals forged in the war still remains strong – photo interpretation, physical training instructors and education. Some act as assistants for combat arms, in particular the Royal Artillery, so preserving another valued association.

The capability of women as staff officers has long been established but something of a landmark is the graduation of one with a master's degree (Msc Econ) in war studies. She has amusingly recounted her intitial difficulties on the drill square, where she performed the classical feat of losing her squad, to find it marking time facing a brick wall. She has the sympathies of many others who have had to learn that difficult art. Here one might interpose the thought that drill and discipline are inseparable. One of the pioneers of forty odd years ago said of volunteer training weeks where women were first introduced to drill we 'used to come in all tituppy on high heels and go out on a Saturday morning making a noise like the whole British army.' But the sweep and breadth of the Corps activities has enabled it to refute, long since, the stereotype of the clumping boots and serge-clad Amazons which has plagued them intermittently since the early days of World War I, but all that is now a matter of history.

It is worth noting that the British model of a woman's service, fully a part of the armed forces, but non-combatant and steering well clear of any offensive action involving the use of weapons, has been widely copied. The Corps has formal links with the Women's Royal Australian Army Corps and the New Zealand Women's Royal Army Corps, and there has long been a close liaison between women's services in all the member countries of the NATO alliance. In 1976 a Committee of Women was set up in official recognition of this, and at the time of writing its chair is held by Brigadier Eileen Nolan, the present Director, Women's Royal Army Corps.

Anyone who follows the fortunes of the British Army will know that the role and scope of all Arms and Services is kept under review. In 1976 a Ministry of Defence working party was set up to consider the future employment of the WRAC. Its scope has been wider than any other on the WRAC since its formation in 1949, and it has sought ways of making a properly balanced and progressive career open to women. The role of, and attitudes to, women have changed markedly, particularly in the last decade, and in the words of the present Adjutant General, Sir Jack Harman, 'We cannot afford to deny the Army, or to employ below their talents, the very high grade young women who are prepared to join the WRAC today.' But a historian is concerned with the past, and it is not his business to speculate on the future. One thing, however, will be agreed by all those who have followed this all too short account, from the days of the 'lady with the frying pan', the first venture overseas, the gallant amateurism of 1939–40, the vast and efficient effort of 1941–45 to the evolution of a regular corps twenty-five years ago: The Women's Royal Army Corps will continue to support the army with the same high professional standards and devotion to duty it has always shown.